Real World
CUSTOMER
SERVICE
STRATEGIES
That
WORK

Insight Publishing Company
Sevierville, Tennessee

Real World
CUSTOMER
SERVICE
STRATEGIES
That
WORK

Suzanne –
Best of luck to you as you help train the finest customer service teams in the world. I hope I can be of value, to you in the process!

Kevin PRullo

"Chapter 2"

Real World
CUSTOMER
SERVICE
STRATEGIES
That
WORK

Published by:
Insight Publishing Company
PO Box 4189
Sevierville, TN 37862

10 9 8 7 6 5 4 3 2

Printed in the United States of America

ISBN 1-885640-82-X

Table Of Contents

A Message From The Publisher

Some of my most rewarding experiences in business—or in my personal life, for that matter—have been at meetings, conventions or gatherings, after the formal events have concluded. Inevitably, small groups of ten to fifteen men and women gather together to rehash the happenings of the day and to exchange war stories, recently heard jokes or the latest gossip from their industry. It is in these informal gatherings where some of the best lessons can be learned.

Usually, in informal groups of professionals, there are those who clearly have lived through more battles and learned more lessons than others. These are the men and women who are really getting the job done, and everyone around the room knows it. When they comment on the topic of the moment, they don't just spout the latest hot theory or trend, and they don't ramble on and on without a relevant point. These battle-scarred warriors have lessons to share that everyone senses are just a little more real, more relevant and therefore, worthy of more attention.

These are the kind of people we have recruited for the *Power Learning* series of books. Each title offers contributions from men and women who are making a significant impact on their culture, in their field, and on their colleagues and clients. This edition offers a variety of themes in the area of customer service strategies. It is ripe with "the good stuff," as an old friend of mine used to always say. Inside these pages you'll find ideas, insights, strategies and philosophies that are working with real people, in real companies and under real circumstances.

It is our hope that you keep this book with you until you've dog-eared every chapter and made so many notes in the margins that you have trouble seeing the original words on the pages. There is treasure here. Enjoy digging!

Chapter One

Achieving Customer Service Excellence: It's More Than Just Being Nice!

Joseph Rosales

Excellent customer service should be a normal occurrence, yet in most retail businesses today, you will, more than likely, not receive exceptional service. Sure, you might receive the product or service you came for, and you may even come in contact with someone who is nice to you. But customer service that exceeds expectations does not occur often enough.

No matter how much we talk about it, the delivery of excellent customer service seems to elude even the most dedicated businesses. Yes, many businesses believe in the importance of providing high levels of customer service and even deliver it on a reasonably consistent basis; however, I think you will agree that positive customer service experiences have become the exception instead of the rule in businesses across the country.

Providing excellent customer service takes planning and execution, and for some, it is more than they are willing to do. But great customer service can be the most exploitable difference between you and your competitors. Virtually anyone can carry the same brands as you, and many are willing to sell for less. However, customers who receive excellent customer service spend more and are typically more loyal to a business than those who receive mediocre service. You will also have fewer customer complaints and spend less time resolving those occasional complaints you do receive.

"Customer service" is a phrase full of promises, but it so often becomes just empty greetings and filling orders. It is interesting that the active word here is "serve," which means to attend to, wait upon, or be a servant to another. In our fast paced society today, we find fewer people willing to submit to each other; however, when it does occur especially in a retail environment, it is noticed and appreciated.

To consistently achieve excellence in customer service requires an integrated approach to providing for a customer that blends good systems and well-planned processes with energetic, friendly, customer-focused people. All showcased in an environment that is attractive and conducive to exceptional service experiences.

Excellent customer service—it's more than just being nice!

As customers, we all experience people who are just going through the motions and activities that make up their jobs. They do their jobs and provide the service, but they don't really do or say anything to make you feel that they care or cause you to feel that it matters to them if you are happy with the service you are receiving.

I am sure you can remember an instance when you were a customer at a business and were being served by an employee who was able to fulfill your request, but was not very nice to you while doing so. I call this behavior "sterile efficiency." Conversely, you can most likely remember a service experience when you were attended to by someone who was nice to you, but could not satisfy the request you came into their business for. Being nice, but unable to help, still equals poor customer service.

In both scenarios, you only received part of what makes up a great customer service experience. From these simple scenarios, you can see how important it is to provide for a customer's primary needs and do so in such a way that he or she feels cared for and appreciated.

To accomplish this simple, but important customer mission, someone has to take the time, have the desire and be in position to make a customer relationship happen. I often hear comments from business owners who say they wish they had time to properly take care of their customers. "I just don't have time," "I'm so understaffed" or "My people won't take time to be friendly". Taking time to develop customer relationships is one of the most underutilized business building skills I see in nearly every segment of retail.

Most often, winning a customer's repeat business is *not* based entirely on the product purchased or service provided. While meeting a customer's expectations for quality products and prompt service are prerequisites to great customer service, no one should be impressed when expectations are simply met.

The simple secrets to excellent customer service

The secrets to achieving excellent customer service are not really secrets at all. They are simply components of your service model. These components I will share with you are all critically important to the mission of achieving excellence in customer service.

- The <u>people</u> who serve your customers and make the relationship more than a transaction
- The <u>environment or facility</u> your customers come to when they purchase products and/or services from you
- The <u>systems and processes</u> that support the experience your customer will receive

It all starts with the right people

The first component of the model for excellent customer service is the people who serve your customers. Who are they? Are they friendly and engaging with customers? Are they properly groomed, and are they motivated to serve customers? Are they the best you could find to work in your business?

In today's competitive labor market, it is becoming harder to find the high-performance, motivated employees every business owner is looking for. However, all good customer service programs succeed because there are employees in place with the right service attitude. So, this first component is vital to the success of the model.

The first step to hiring the right people to serve your customers is to develop a clear vision for the type of people you want working in your business. Think about this statement: "You can't make orange juice with lemons." So it is, with trying to make happy customers with unfriendly employees.

Begin the vision process by imagining the friendly, pleasant, enthusiastic people you would like to have staffing your business. Grooming, speech, attitude and the desire to excel and be part of a winning team are key traits that you should include in your employee profile. Don't overlook the fact that the image that you personally project to your customers is very often imitated by your employees in their own customer interactions. So have the right service attitude yourself.

The exercise of writing out the character traits and skills you are looking for in an employee will help you establish the foundation for recruiting the best employees to work with you in your business. As you develop a vision of the ideal employees you are looking for, you will notice them working at other businesses and will begin to see employee candidates in a new light. You will also start to set your expectations higher.

Surely, different positions in different industries may require specific skill sets; however, the single common trait shared by all successful employees in a customer-focused business is a good attitude. A very simple yet powerful rule in hiring people is: "Hire attitude; train competence." You can teach almost anyone how to follow the procedures that will result in the consistent and technically correct delivery of your product or service. But it is very difficult, if not impossible, to teach someone to have the right attitude and to be friendly.

Where do you find these excellent people? They are out there, although most of them are already working for someone else. But don't lose faith. Be open to the idea that you can still find highly motivated employees to work for you. Although we hear every day that businesses just can't find good employees, I still find employees serving customers with excellence and having a great time doing it.

All this is easily said, but it is often harder to do. But no one ever said that delivering world-class customer service would be easy. If it were easy, everyone would be doing it already, and you wouldn't need to read this book!

Great customer service is everyone's responsibility

My wife is a great barometer for most customer service businesses. Once, when I asked her to tell me what she thought represented good customer service, she said without hesitation, "When someone looks like he enjoys his job."

As I thought about her comment, I immediately had a vision of an employee who, when asked by a customer how his day is going, responds with, "My day will be great in about thirty minutes, when I finish my shift." Doesn't that say the employee would rather be somewhere else instead of serving the customer's needs? Conversely, when you come in contact with someone who likes his job, he is normally happy, enthusiastic and smiling! Are we always going to feel happy? I don't think so, but we can always respond to a customer like we do.

Everyone on your staff should understand the importance of customer relations and providing superior service. And although every member of your staff is responsible for developing and maintaining positive customer relationships, someone needs to be in position to be sure every customer interaction is positive and adds to the customers' experience.

Image—does it really matter?

The second component of excellent customer service is the environment your customers visit to purchase your products or services. Does the appearance and cleanliness of the environment speak quality and organization? Is the environment properly merchandised? What printed messages are the customers exposed to, and do they support informing and educating the customer about your products and services? Is the customer restroom spotless? These and many other environmental issues create impressions on your customers. Will the impressions your customers receive be positive, or negative ?

As both a consultant and a customer, I often find myself saying "Wow" when I come in contact with businesses. Sometimes, the "Wow" is a positive response when I'm visiting a business that has obviously created its environment to make a positive impression on its customers. Sometimes the "Wow" is not positive when I see businesses that have put zero thought into how their environment impacts the customer.

Properly imaging an environment speaks to the many details that must be attended to in order to make a customer comfortable in your business. From clean restrooms, to soft background music, to the chair a customer sits in. Every point in the interior and exterior your customer comes in contact with at your business needs to be planned and carefully controlled.

The Exterior

Exterior signage is critical to letting your customers know that your business even exists. Equally important is the message it conveys to your customer beyond the words on the sign. For example, is the signage well kept and clean? Is it well lighted? Does it effectively add to the image of your business in such a way that it invites and inspires a customer to come inside?

Landscaping is another imaging point. Is your landscaping well maintained? Have you taken advantage of opportunities to use color in the landscape design? Are there flowers, mulch and shrubs? If you have a lawn, is it green and healthy, or is it dead? Are there more weeds than grass? Is litter strewn about? A well-manicured exterior speaks volumes to a customer about what she might expect inside the business.

I remember reading a story about Ray Kroc, the founder of the McDonald's restaurant chain. Legend has it that even in his later years, Mr. Kroc would have his driver stop his car near a McDonald's he was visiting. Mr. Kroc would then proceed to personally pick up every piece of paper he saw along the way. He felt strongly about keeping the grounds around the restaurants free of litter, or anything else that would distract from the visual appeal of the business. He would take the bag full of papers and trash, march right into the manager's office and set it on his desk. Not much else needed to be said, as I am sure his point was made. I admired Mr. Kroc for his commitment to cleanliness and his dramatic way of making his point.

Lighting at night is also important for many businesses. If your business is located outside, guess what? During most of the year it is dark for as many hours as it is daylight. If your facility is not properly lit at night, then thousands of potential customers who normally only travel by your location at night are oblivious to the fact that your business even exists.

The Interior

While decorating a business's interior can reflect one's personal tastes, there are some imaging basics that must be adhered to. Beyond purely cosmetic elements like wallpaper and paint, a well-designed imaging package will address many other issues, including customer comfort and education. The proper imaging and merchandising touches will not only make for a more attractive environment but also will also directly affect sales of additional products and services.

Consider some of the following suggestions when reviewing your own interior imaging program:

- If your business requires that customers be seated for a period of time, make sure they will be comfortable. The nature of your business will dictate to a certain degree the type of seating you can use; however, a few basics apply here as well. The upholstery on the seats should be a medium color that will not show dirt and normal wear and tear.

- Consider using direct lighting to highlight specific interior signs, which will help bring attention to the message being communicated. Make sure your interior is neither too light nor too dark. Lighting can make a big difference in how your business appears to your customers, yet it is a very subtle issue that is overlooked by most businesses.

- Plants can be an inexpensive way to add a touch of class and create a more inviting environment in a business. To test the importance of this concept, try removing the plants from a room in your house for an afternoon and see how bare it appears. You might, however, avoid the maintenance issue that comes with real plants and use silk plants instead. A quality silk plant can look real and require no upkeep other than an occasional dusting.

- For customers who care (and most do), the cleanliness of the restrooms is very important. The impression it conveys can make or break the other image components. Try to create an environment that is clean without being too sterile and warm without being too fluffy. Use wallpaper on at least one wall (commercial grade that is easily cleaned). Add a silk flower/plant arrangement for color. Make sure to have all the paper products a customer would need, along with soap and air freshener. And don't use the restroom as a storage closet!

A few words on uniforms

Recently, the largest regional bank in our area put all of its tellers in blue sweater vests that displayed the bank logo. The officers and account representatives are not outfitted in them, of course, since they are required to wear suits. However, the sight of these well attired tellers serving their customers was very impressive. The uniform look standardized the imaging behind the counter and made the tellers look more professional; it even made the rest of the decor more complete. It also minimized the issue that many businesses face of their employees all wearing their own individual style of clothing and presenting a less than professional image. The right uniform, worn well and maintained properly, conveys professionalism and organization.

Uniforms can have many different looks, from a pressed and starched shirt and slacks to a more casual golf shirt and cotton pants. Every business has to decide for itself what works for its specific environment. One thing is for sure—uniforms should be uniform. The word "uniform" essentially means sameness or similarity—all coordinated, all the same.

Let me share an "imaging incident" that happened to me recently. I needed an oil change for my car, so I stopped at an oil change facility that is close to our corporate offices. I had never had my oil changed there before. I pulled up to one of the open bays, and after about thirty seconds, a young man approached my car. I was not sure if he worked there or not, since he was not wearing a uniform. In fact, what he was wearing surprised me: a faded blue T-shirt with a huge hole in it, his paunchy, hairy belly showing through. The shirt was not tucked in and as is the style with many young people nowadays, his jeans were at least three to four waist sizes too big, with the crotch hanging down around his knees. Not the kind of uniform presentation that projected professionalism.

Clearly, some customers don't treat an oil change as a very important issue and will let anyone service their car. This is evidenced by competitors that perform poor quality work, but still get plenty of customers because they are cheaper or because the customers just want an oil change and don't really care who does it. However, that is not how I and many other customers feel.

I did not get my oil changed at that business. And my decision was not based on their actual ability to perform the service as much as my feelings about how they might deal with me, or a problem with my car. Certainly, if the owner of this facility did not care enough to provide proper uniforms and training to his employee, then I certainly did not want to be on the opposing end of a service problem with him. Based on this initial impression, I had no reason to believe that anyone else on the staff would be any better. I could not risk getting my car serviced there.

Perception is not reality

I am sure you have heard the old adage "perception is reality." That isn't really true. My perception was that this technician was not experienced and that he and the owner did not care. The truth could very well have been that the technician was very experienced and that the owner cared a great deal. However, I will never learn the truth.

How could my visit have gone differently? To start, the technician greeting me should have been in a proper uniform. Someone working on my car wearing a ripped up T-shirt does not inspire feelings of confidence. Second, the tech should have been trained how to properly greet customers and present the service in a friendly and engaging manner. In this scenario, my initial perception became reality and dictated that I not get my car serviced at this facility. What do customers see when they come to your business?

Educating and informing your customers

In today's business environment, it has become increasingly important to offer a wider range of services and products. This is driven not only by the obvious need to generate more revenue per customer but also by the consumer who wants and needs more services and asks that you fulfill those needs.

With more choices for your customers comes the challenge of properly merchandising the various offerings you provide in a way that is clear and evident to your customers. An effectively merchandised environment is not only more attractive, but it also helps to educate your customer about the services you can provide for him.

The more your customer understands about your business, the better prepared he is to make the right decisions. The owner and spokesperson of a successful chain of clothing stores says it best: "Our best customer is an educated consumer."

I feel that the education of our customers is another of the most overlooked aspects of many service businesses. Maybe one of the reasons is that we assume customers know and understand the range of services and products we offer. Interviews with customers indicate that the majority of customers know very little about the businesses they frequent and less about the services these businesses offer.

Obviously, one of the most effective methods for sharing information with a customer is good, old-fashioned conversation. In addition to the verbal communications you are having with customers, there are two other communications points you should focus on—store signage and displays. This typically includes wall signage, brochures, banners and product displays.

Signage and displays are often called the "silent sales person." Effective signage and displays can often account for ten to fifteen percent of sales and can further support the sales efforts of virtually every service and product you offer.

The objective of properly developed signage and displays should be to educate with the intent of supporting a customer's decision to purchase a service or product. If you have ever had a customer approach you and ask for a service because he or she read about it on a sign or brochure, then you have experienced the benefits of effective signage. Now you just need to make that happen more often.

Don't just communicate the message with signage. Imagine walking into a grocery store and just seeing signage for fruits and vegetables, with no photos or real items displayed. Would you buy apples based only on a sign that said "apples" and then let the store ship them to you at home later? Most people would not. We want to *see* the apple before we buy it. People are visual by nature. We more easily buy what we can see or touch.

Many of our clients use custom-designed videotapes or DVD's to educate customers. This medium is simple yet interactive and, therefore, more powerful. Customers who are waiting for services are a captive audience for a video that talks about a company's newest or most popular products or services. A video may not necessarily sell the customer on the spot, but it could very well plant the seed for buying a product or service on a subsequent visit.

In whatever manner you decide to inform and educate your customers, keep it fresh. Change the signage and displays periodically. Sometimes, the same signage, rotated to a different location within the store, will give you a new look and yield new opportunities.

Certainly there are many other issues we could discuss related to the exterior and interior of a retail business environment. However, the planning and preparing that goes into creating an environment that is attractive, comfortable and informative for your customers is paramount to good customer service.

Systems and processes support the service experience

I have heard people say that excellent customer service is quickly becoming a lost art in retail businesses. I believe the best customer service is less art and more process. Let me explain further;

Systems are tools to support the process, like a POS computer system that maintains a customer's information, needs or buying habits. Processes are the steps that outline how we can best serve a customer in an efficient, effective and personalized way.

Certainly, your employees are the main interface with your customers and make the systems and processes personalized and relevant to the customers' needs. However, without the systems and processes in place, each customer's interaction with your business will be different and subsequently have the potential for not meeting his or her need for consistency. The comfort that comes with consistency is lost, and the customer may not know what to expect on future visits. Consistency builds repeat businesses.

For some, creating the systems and processes is the most challenging aspect of the service model. But rest easy; capturing the perfect customer interaction and creating a series of processes that can be used as a model to recreate the interaction again and again, is actually quite easy and will yield returns many times the invested hours.

Some initial things to consider: How are your customers greeted? What specific words best help welcome and orient them to your business? Certainly, there are more appropriate and effective greetings to use when greeting a customer than simply asking, "Can I help you?" Depending on the environment you are in, the customer is likely to just say, "No. I am just looking." And a rule in greeting a customer is "never greet a customer with a greeting they can say "no" to as a response. Always greet a customer with a "Hello" followed by a statement which will open a dialogue or conversation.

Every customer contact, conversation or product explanation needs to be reviewed, planned and practiced to assure that you are properly and accurately communicating to a customer. Whether it is handling a product inquiry or a customer complaint, the words you use make impressions on customers and cause them to respond accordingly. Don't leave any communications up to chance.

What is the best presentation of your business? How do you communicate about additional products and services you offer? Are you trying to sell to your customers, or are you qualifying needs, counseling and presenting information? How do you explain your guarantees? Make sure your staff knows how to communicate how your business is different than the competition.

Friendly and engaging—the missing ingredient

One should not understand processes to be sterile, non-personal interactions. On the contrary, the processes I envision for businesses are very friendly and engaging. Yet they also allow for the unique processes of your business model to be addressed with every customer and ensure that the experience of being your customer is more predicable and easier to duplicate for your staff.

As a society, we continue to make everything faster and more automated. In fact, certain industries are on a path to automate much of the personal contact right out of their business. From banks to gas stations to convenience stores, we see computer technology enabling people to handle basic deposits and withdrawals, fill up their cars with gas and order lunch without ever coming in direct contact with a person.

At one point, many people thought retail branch banking would go the way of full automation. It didn't. Customers still want to talk to a person when they open an account and certainly if they are reviewing investment opportunities. Fortunately, people serving people will always be part of the customer service equation. Even with Internet-based companies, the promise of service is made by a person and ultimately kept or broken by a person.

The phrase "customer service" is overused in business, to the point that it almost seems to have lost its meaning. I have to believe that in its earliest usage, it must have referred to serving customers. Somewhere along the line, we must have flipped it around to the point that it is focused less on serving customers and more on processing transactions.

The value of a smile

As I visit clients in various parts of the world, I am always reminded that no matter what language is spoken, a smile is a universal and powerful communication tool. A friendly smile is a great way to show someone that you are glad he has come to your business. Often, we find that employees and managers who come in contact with customers are not aware of how much impact their facial expressions have on customers' experiences at their business.

Think about it. Would you rather do business with someone who is friendly, engaging and smiling or someone who is a grouch? Sometimes, a person feels happy on the inside but doesn't show it, so he doesn't smile, and he looks unhappy. Customers can't read minds, but they can read a smile.

Here are some interesting facts about smiles:

- Smiles are free.
- Smiles don't take any extra time.
- You have an unlimited supply of smiles.
- When you give a smile, you usually get one in return.
- Smiles make the "smile-er" and the "smile-ee" feel good.

Smile...it's good for business and good for your health!

"Thank you" and "My pleasure"

When a customer asks, "How are you today?" she is usually just making conversation and being polite. She is not asking for a story of woe. The reply should not be anything except "Great," "Fantastic," "Good" or any other positive exclamation. It should also be followed by, "And how are you?" Certainly, I am not suggesting that you should tell a customer you are fabulous when you are not. But we should understand the purpose of the question and be tactful in our responses.

When a customer says "thank you," what is the response from your staff? Most of the time, I hear "No problem." I understand what someone means when he responds that way, but think about it. Is that the most gracious response? The proper response should always be "My pleasure" or simply "You are welcome."

Are you already giving every customer the friendly service and smiles he or she deserves? Are you saying and doing the things that let your customers know that you truly appreciate them—not just those you like but even those whom you don't know? When you are in front of a customer, it's show time. Enthusiasm, friendliness and smiles should all be part of the presentation.

Caring is an imperative

Most customers don't care how much you know, but they need to know how much you care. Customers don't always expect you to have the right answer, or to always be perfect in your business; however, they do need to know that you care about helping them. If you don't know the answer to the customer's inquiry, you must display an attitude that you care and will find out the proper information and apply a proper solution.

Here is an interesting statistic: The number one reason a customer will stop doing business with a business is an attitude of indifference shown by an employee. This can easily be displayed to a customer by simply not being attentive, not stopping what he is doing while the customer is talking, or even appearing to be preoccupied. Indifference can show up at any time and needs to be guarded against at all times.

One simple method to display an attentive attitude is to always make eye contact with a customer while conversing, and occasionally nod your head or use a word of acknowledgement to let her know you are listening.

A customer service hero...the "Ritz" experience

Let me share a story about one of my customer service heroes. This particular one is actually a group of people. The experience I will share with you demonstrates perfectly how the right people, equipped with the right systems and processes, framed in the right environment, will produce customer service excellence.

During the course of my business life, I have stayed at some of the finest hotels in the world. However, none to this day compares with the experience my wife and I had during a recent stay at the Ritz Carlton in Key Biscayne, Florida.

From the moment we arrived at the front door, the excellent service began. The valet staff was attentive and extremely polite. When I said "Thank you," their reply was "It is my pleasure." How simple and sweet those words were; not "No problem" or some other, less-than-gracious reply but simply "It is my pleasure."

What occurred over the next three days was an experience that not only impressed, but inspired. I expected much of it; the well-groomed staff, the immaculate landscaping, the beautifully decorated and well-appointed rooms. Sure, the beautiful ocean view and warm breezes were priceless, but nothing could match the attitude, enthusiasm and personal care my wife and I received from the staff.

The people were not just well groomed, but perfectly attired. Even the maids looked as though every hair was in place, and their uniforms were perfectly pressed. Everyone made an effort to greet us no matter what his or her job was. From towel boy or landscaper to air conditioning technician, everyone greeted us with a friendly hello. You expect this kind of engagement from the valet, desk staff or pool attendants, but not from everyone else. Everyone had a serving attitude, a sparkle in their eyes. When we chose to chat with a waiter, they were ready to engage in conversation. When we chose to have privacy, they were never intrusive. It was perfect.

I could write a book about the attentiveness shown to the hotel's environment. The colors, the furnishings, the textures were all tastefully done and timeless. The room temperature was not too hot and not too cold. Everything smelled fresh, and every detail was attended to. At turn-down service, they even place a fine linen mat at bedside, so that when you awoke in the morning, your feet would not touch carpet but a soft, crisp, linen mat. This was just another of the many details they attended to with one objective in mind—to impress their guests and provide the ultimate in comfort and service.

Through the use of the simplest technology of headsets and two-way radios, they went the extra mile to assure their guests received the best service and their staff members were equipped to access information and communicate with each other in the quest for service excellence.

When on vacation with my wife and family, I plan that we will receive excellent service and enjoy every moment of the time we spend together. I do not leave to chance the possibility of poor service, or poor accommodations. The Ritz Carlton in Key Biscayne exceeded my expectations at a level I have rarely experienced. Without a doubt, when in South Florida, we will return to this hotel.

Quite simply, they combined sharp, engaging people with a service attitude. Management provided them with a facility that is carefully thought out and imaged to the highest standards of quality. And they equipped their staff with the right systems and processes that will allow them to exceed their guests expectations. Beautiful in its simplicity, but very difficult to compete with.

Are there other hotels that can match up? I am sure there are others that can and do achieve this level of total customer service excellence. If you are thinking that you are not the Ritz Carlton, that's okay; you don't have to be. What I am speaking of here are standards of excellence that anyone can attain if they are willing to have a vision and do what it takes to attain it.

Too often, businesses deliver customer service that is less than they could achieve, because management sets the standard too low. Set the bar high for your customer service expectations. Keep the bar high, and you will more than likely attain excellent customer service more often.

Each and every contact with a customer matters, but it takes more than just a smile and a "thank you" to ensure good customer service. As I like to say and often do, Customer Service is a Contact Sport™.

If there is a best way, there is a worst way

If there is a way to do anything, there are best ways and there are worst ways. The most successful business operators will always seek the best way to do things. They will hire the best staff to serve their customers, create the most attractive environment and seek out the best systems and processes that will serve the customer with an attitude that is individualized, personalized and energized.

So you see, excellent customer service is really the result of careful planning and execution. It starts with the selection, training and development of the people who serve your customers. It continues with the planning and design of the environment in which the customer will be served. Guide the interactions between customers and your staff with well-conceived systems and processes, and if you are disciplined in keeping the vision, customer service magic happens. It's really a thing of beauty.

I bid you well in your quest for customer service excellence.

About The Author

Joseph Rosales

Joseph Rosales is the founder and president of Customer Service Solutions, Inc (CSS), an international consulting and training firm that specializes in helping companies improve customer service and employee performance. CSS offers a wide range of services to their clients, from assessing current service processes to improvement consultation and training. Joseph's book *Customer Service is a Contact Sport*™ has revolutionized the way businesses look at customer service. It is also available in CD and audiotape formats. Also available as a keynote address, breakout session and a series of integrated workshops, *Customer Service is a Contact Sport*™ can provide you with the insight and processes you need to achieve customer service excellence.

Joseph Rosales
Customer Service Solutions, Inc.
560 Stokes Road, Suite 23-373
Medford, NJ 08055
Phone: 1.800.268.9899
Fax: 856.988.0807
Email: jrosales@customerservicesolutions.com
Web: www.customerservicesolutions.com

Chapter Two

Leadership: The Ultimate Customer Service Multiplier

Kevin R. Miller

"On the battlefield, leadership is a force multiplier." I will never forget the moment I first heard this statement, as a young Army lieutenant in officer basic training. It came from the lips of a hardened, experienced, combat-veteran master sergeant. In the twenty-plus years I have spent developing military, corporate and academic leaders, I am now more convinced than ever: Not only is leadership *a* "force multiplier," it is *the* greatest force multiplier you can apply to any system.

Of course, the applications of this statement on the battlefield are obvious. The leadership of Robert E. Lee and Thomas "Stonewall" Jackson was a force multiplier for an undermanned, inexperienced and under-equipped Confederate army in the first eighteen months of our Civil War. (Had the Union army been blessed with this caliber of leaders, the war would have probably ended in six months.) George Washington, George S. Patton, Napoleon, Alexander—all were force multipliers on the battlefield. But in a very real sense, we are all engaged in battlefields of our own as we tackle the tests of leading ourselves, our families and our organizations against a formidable array of challenges.

It is suitable that this chapter is near the start of this book, because leadership is the greatest force multiplier you need in building a world-class customer service program. I will present six force multipliers you can use in achieving this vision.

Heroes and Zeros

As I go about delivering my "Customers Only Want Two Things" service training, I enjoy playing the "heroes and zeros" game. I ask participants to share experiences they have had—as customers receiving "hero" service and "zero" service from business establishments—ranking them on a ten-point scale. We've all had them. I'll share two of my favorites, a zero story of my own and a hero story I heard from someone else.

My zero story:

On a warm, summer day in 1996, I went to grab a quick lunch at Hardee's, a fast-food outlet in Provo, Utah. As I walked up to place my order, I was greeted with what I call "the rolling-eyed glare" of a young, blonde seventeen year old. (Sometimes, I wonder if teenagers attend some special training to learn how to roll their eyes disgustedly!) Her attitude was clear but unspoken: "This would be a pretty good place to work if these stupid customers didn't keep coming in the door." I ordered a combo meal and a chocolate shake. She glared, shoved my tray at me and took my money. When I sat down, I gagged on discovering that the chocolate shake was warm! I took it back to the girl, who glared again and asked, "What's the problem?" I told her, and she stuck her finger in the shake, wiped it on her apron and sighed. She then proceeded to fiddle around with the shake machine and said, "I'll have to talk to the manager." She disappeared and returned a couple of minutes later with her "boss," who turned out to be an equally dozy eye roller. He said, "What's your problem?" (This showed me that the girl didn't even care enough to pass on my complaint to him.) We went through the same process as he fiddled with the machine then said, "So what do you want?" I said, "Another drink, I guess," and he said, "Well, you can't have a shake!" (I thought, "Well, duhhhh!") He shoved an empty cup at me and gestured to the drink dispenser. As I walked back to my cold hamburger and limp, greasy fries, I was steaming. I turned around and said in a loud voice, "I will *never* eat at Hardee's again." Almost in concert, they rolled their eyes as if in synch and offered lopsided grins as if to say, "So?" And you know what? I've never darkened a Hardee's door again, and I never will. If I were dying of hunger, dragging myself down the street with bloody fingers and Hardee's were the first joint I came to, I'd just keep on crawlin'.

Now compare this to a remarkable hero story shared by Valerie Oberle, vice president of Disney University guest programs. She has told this story to audiences and also shared it in the book *Chicken Soup for the Soul at Work*.

A hero story:

A lady guest was checking out of Walt Disney World's Polynesian Village Resort in Florida. She'd had a great time but told the front-desk hostess that she was heartbroken over losing some rolls of film, most particularly the shots of the Polynesian Luau. The hostess asked her to leave a couple of rolls of fresh film. Two weeks later, this guest received in the mail a package containing new photos of Disney World, including the parade and shots of the entire cast of the Luau, personally autographed by the performers! These photos had been taken by the front-desk hostess after work, on her own time. Valerie saw the letter this guest wrote, in which she said that never in her life had she received such compassionate service from any business.

I was astonished by this story. That a front-desk hostess, serving hundreds of people a day, would care enough to go that extra mile for someone is almost mind-boggling. Valerie said, "Heroic service does not come from policy manuals. It comes from people who care—and from a culture that encourages and models that attitude."

There is a gulf of difference between the zeros at Hardee's that day and the anonymous hero at Disney World. Obviously, much can be attributed to the character of the individuals involved. However, I also attribute much of it to the force multiplier of leadership—leadership that created the culture to which Valerie referred.

**Is your service program a Hero
or a Zero?**

Now I ask you to be honest with yourself as you analyze your service program. In my seminars, I stretch a ten-foot piece of paper across a wall and write "zero" at one end, "hero" at the other and draw a one-to-ten scale in between. I ask participants to place a check mark along the scale as if they were one of your customers. I usually see votes all across the paper, with the most ratings grouped in the six to seven range. But is this all our customers deserve? Is seventy percent good enough to be world class? Will seventy percent keep your customers coming back again and again? Let us apply the force multipliers of leadership to cross this gulf.

THE SIX FORCE MULTIPLIERS OF CUSTOMER SERVICE LEADERSHIP

While these are not necessarily in order, there are six major force multipliers that leaders can apply as they build world-class customer service programs. After each one, I invite you to use the ten-point scale to evaluate your own program.

Force Multiplier # 1: The Power of a Compelling Vision

President Ronald Reagan once said, *"To grasp and hold a vision, to fix it in your senses, that is the very essence, I believe, of successful leadership."* I could not agree more. Great organizations, be they families, businesses or nations, are focused on a compelling vision, a vision that ignites and unifies the hearts of all engaged in it, a vision that makes you tremble when you read it and makes you want to live it.

Before manufacturing his first Model T, Henry Ford began with the end in mind, with a clear, concise vision:

"I will build a car for the great multitude. It will be large enough for the family but small enough for the individual to run and care for. It will be constructed of the best materials, by the best men to be hired, after the simplest designs that modern engineering can devise. But it will be low in price so that no man making a good salary will be unable to own one—and enjoy with his family the blessing of hours of pleasure in God's great open spaces."

Henry Ford's vision statement contains all the elements I use when I go into organizations to facilitate their creating corporate vision and mission statements. It is *concise, clear, compelling* and *measurable*. It engages the hearts of those who read it. It provides a crystal clear picture of what the end must be. Most of all, it drove everything that Ford did in the early days. When the current process of making cars was too expensive to realize his vision, Henry challenged the process and refined the assembly line system to the point that Model Ts were selling for less than $300. That is the power of a vision.

My friend, Dr. Stephen R. Covey, says that,

> "Leadership is the creation of a culture or a relationship surrounding a common vision."

I propose that the original vision of Walt Disney, even though he is long dead, created the culture that helped inspire that front desk hostess to be such a hero that day.

> Walt Disney said, "We will do what we do so well that the people who see it will want to see it again and bring friends."

With more than forty million visitors to his Orlando theme park each year, Disney obviously succeeded.

Great leaders unite their teams in a process called "co-missioning." Great visions and missions are best created when as many people as possible are involved in their inception. This process can also be called "pathfinding," which, more simply stated, is linking what the folks out there are passionate to get with what your organization and people are passionate to give. Disney applies the power of pathfinding in one of its basic mission statements: *"We create happiness by providing the finest in entertainment to people of all ages everywhere."* Examine this mission statement and compare it to your own. In just fifteen words, Disney creates a compelling vision that not only tells what they do but, more importantly, why. They link *what* they are passionate to give (fine entertainment) with what their customers are passionate to get (happiness).

I have worked with dozens of organizations to help them create mission and vision statements that do what Disney did with theirs. Usually, I find mission statements that are cumbersome, wordy, uninspiring and completely forgettable. They are framed and stuck on a wall somewhere gathering dust. I will share a couple of examples of how a mission statement can evolve.

1. I was working with a movie theater to help them create a compelling and exciting mission. Their previous mission statement was "framed whatever" that read something like this:

"Our mission is to provide our customers with a positive movie-going experience and to develop and nurture our employees by providing them with a clean theater, top quality, new-release movies and blah, blah, blah."

You've heard this stuff before, right?

After a little work, they came up with one that was quite a bit better (at least shorter!):

"We guarantee top-quality movie-going experiences to our valued customers by providing superb, recent-release movie entertainment in an uplifting, positive environment, in the cleanest theater in the valley."

But this still did not connect what they were passionate to give with what customers were passionate to get. It was missing the critical "why" piece. We went back to work and created the final version:

> "We provide refreshment for the soul by pro-
> viding a complete movie experience in the
> finest theater in Utah Valley."

We do this through:
- Maintaining the cleanest theater in the region
- Treating every customer like family
- Our friendly, family atmosphere
- Smiling at and personally greeting every patron
- Offering unique services
- Remembering that the little things are the big things

Can you see, and better yet, feel the difference? The final statement captured the deeper purpose of their mission and provided some
specific ways to do it. By using the bullets beneath, they did not jum-
ble up the main statement and kept it at nineteen words. My
challenge to you is to create, in twenty words or less, a compelling
mission that uplifts, excites and unites every stakeholder who reads
it.

2. My second example is even more interesting. I was working with a
financial planning and financial services company in California. Their
mission statement was a lengthy, mumbo-jumbo mess of financial
jargon about a page long. I kept drilling them to understand exactly
what they offered their customers: "Why do people hunger for financial services such as retirement planning, saving for college and
insurance?" In the end, we created a six-word statement that said it
all:

> "We let you sleep at night."

Now this statement is probably more of a vision statement, because it doesn't say anything about what they do. However, what a
great marketing slogan! In fact, they plan to make billboards that
just have those six words and their company name on them. To translate it into a mission statement, they might do this:

"We let you sleep at night by solving your
financial planning concerns."

Now that you understand this concept, I must ask the tough question: How does your mission statement measure up?

Our mission statement is:

Cumbersome, wordy, uninspiring, forgettable.	1 2 3 4 5 6 7 8 9 10	Compelling, crisp, exciting, focused and useful.
Unknown to most people, rarely used to make decisions or drive action.	1 2 3 4 5 6 7 8 9 10	Known and used by all to drive action and attitudes.

If you contact me, I will be delighted to assist your organization in unleashing the power of this force multiplier by leading you through a special process I have created.

Force Multiplier # 2: The Power of Engagement

The lesson here is clear: You can have the most compelling and exciting mission statement in the world, but if you don't drill it deep into the culture of your organization and into the hearts, minds and actions of your team, it is worth only the paper you printed it on.

When I visit organizations, I play a fun little game. Hiding a full squirt gun behind my back, I ask, "Do you have a company mission statement?" Usually, everyone proudly nods. I then pull the squirt gun out, point it at the CEO or top manager and ask "What is it?" They usually gasp, struggle, cough out a word or two—and then get soaked. I then move down the line, and by the time I get to the end, everyone is sprayed. I did this with a team one year after I had led them through the process of creating a very good mission statement. Sadly, I ended up spraying every chagrined person except one—the secretary who had typed it so many times that she had it memorized! (By the way, consider yourself warned if you ever invite me to visit you!)

I am fairly certain that this would not happen at a world-class organization like Disneyland or Walt Disney World. Why? Because they spend a great deal of time instilling in every employee the underlying vision, values and mission of Disney. I heard once that Disney leaders were shocked to discover that the average seventeen-year-old job applicant at Disneyland did not even know that there was once a real person named Walt Disney; they knew nothing about him, his dream or what he created. After all, they were born long after Disney's TV show, hosted by Walt himself, was off the air. This inspired Disney to create its famous orientation program, in which each employee learns about the history of Disney's dream and what the real values and purposes of Disney are. They are then "put into costume" and sent out to serve, even if it is as a street sweeper on Main Street U.S.A. They know their mission is to make people happy, not simply sweep streets.

Another great example is the Ritz Carlton hotel chain, which has repeatedly won honors as the top luxury-class leader in its field. It created a vision/slogan for its employees:

"We are ladies and gentlemen,
serving ladies and gentlemen."

And then there's the Ritz Carlton credo:

"The Ritz-Carlton Hotel is a place where the genuine care and comfort of our guests is our highest mission. We pledge to provide the finest personal service and facilities for our guests, who will always enjoy a warm, relaxed yet refined experience."

They then proceed to drill this slogan and credo deep into every employee by repeatedly training him or her on their steps of service. Everyone carries a tri-fold card that contains the slogan, the credo and the steps of service.

So once you have a vision (Force Multiplier #1), how do you engage everyone to bring it to fruition? I have some suggestions:

First, communicate it, communicate it and communicate it some more! Have everyone memorize it.

- Print it on the back of business cards. (And give every single employee business cards; it makes them feel that they belong! Hint: Just get the Avery perforated laser business cards, and whip them out as needed.)
- Put it on the header or footer of all internal memos, documents and meeting agendas so it can be referred to in all deliberations.
- Recite the vision or mission frequently.
- Role play how to live the mission. My daughter worked for a fast-food place that had the employees team up to create a skit, a song and a battle-cry around its mission statement. She never forgot the statement!

Second, empower and resource people to be able to instantly live the mission. There is a statement that says, "When really good people run into really bad processes, the bad processes almost always win." I find that most organizations are misaligned. Out of one side of their mouth they talk customer service, but then they disempower the first-line employees to the point where they cannot possibly walk the talk. This institutionalized mistrust and disempowerment hurts, disillusions and disheartens people.

For example, the young girl serving me in my zero Hardee's story evidently did not have enough authority or training to be able to instantly solve my problem with a new drink, fresh, hot food or a "bounce-back" coupon inviting me to return for a free meal. She had to go to her manager to get his approval for an action that cost almost nothing.

Compare this to the Ritz Carlton, which gives every single employee a generous "blank check" that they can use to instantly satisfy a customer without any management approval. They can waive a room fee, give free meals or desserts, you name it. What does this tell the employee? It says, "We trust you and give you ownership over the customer experience. Do what you have to do within this dollar limit, using your best judgment. Make it happen!" Even if an occasional misjudgment or misuse occurs, the Ritz Carlton knows that the payback in terms of employee empowerment, ownership and customer satisfaction is well worth it. And it is; the Ritz Carlton consistently enjoys the highest customer satisfaction marks in its class as well as the lowest customer complaint ratio.

Here are a few suggestions:

- Establish the dollar range mentioned in the example above.
- Train your employees on how to satisfy customer problems. Remember, if you try to motivate people without training them, you only frustrate them!
- Establish a set of clear standards and steps of service.
- Create a list of Frequently Asked Questions (FAQ) and their Frequently Given Responses (FGR), and thoroughly train every employee in how to use them.

Third, catch people in the act of doing things right. Recognize and reward examples of living the mission. The old adage, "You get what you reward" rings true in the service environment. As a leader, get in the habit of watching for instances where your employees live the mission and deliver what it promises. To do this, you may have to symbolically grow two new eyeballs that only see the good things (your old eyeballs are well trained to see only the problems!). Try to catch your employees doing things right, and instantly recognize them. These recognitions need not be expensive. Simple gestures of specific, timely thanks and small things like candy or movie passes will do the trick.

In working with organizations, I find that most of them have some pathetic employee-of-the-month program or other reward system as their only carrot. These programs have proven to have little or no value whatsoever in motivating a change in behavior. In study after study, the things employees state they want the most at work are recognition for work well done and feeling as if they are "in on things."

In an instance at the Mirage Hotel in Las Vegas, inspired leaders reduced the annual turnover of their housekeeping staff from 200 percent to about seventeen percent over a two-year period by constantly recognizing work well done with simple, engraved poker chips that could be redeemed for gifts at the gift store. These chips had more intrinsic than extrinsic value; in fact, the employees rarely redeemed them. Remember, the "warm fuzzy versus cold prickly" story?

Here are some other suggestions:

- Involve customers in recognizing great service. One hotel gives each customer a "gold coin" to award employees who do a particularly good job.

- Have a peer-recognition program where peers can catch fellow employees doing something well, submit a "caught-ya card" and also be recognized for doing so.
- Create a unique "pass along" award that can travel from employee to employee as they catch each other performing great service. I recently visited a university bookstore that created a "Spam" (Super Positive Attitude Master) award. They mounted a can of Spam on a trophy, created a Spam T-shirt and passed the trophy around to recognize great acts of service. Fantastic.
- Read the book *A Thousand and One Ways to Reward Employees* by Bob Nelson for dozens of low-cost, innovative ways to reward others. Another great book is *The 24 Carrot Manager,* by Adrian Gostick.

So how would you rate yourself in Force Multiplier #2?

How well are our people empowered?

Our processes encumber, disempower and disable our employees.	1 2 3 4 5 6 7 8 9 10	Our processes allow maximum flexibility and empowerment to our employees.
Our employees are not trained well enough in how to satisfy customer wants and what their options are.	1 2 3 4 5 6 7 8 9 10	Our training provides concrete tools and guidelines on how to serve our customers.

Force Multiplier # 3: The Power of Recruiting the Right Folks

I can't overstate the value of making the right hires. Almost every leader has made the mistake of hiring the wrong person, personality-wise, into a service position. Southwest Airlines, which is famous for its friendly, energetic staff, has a simple credo: Hire for personality and train for skill. (I hope they don't do this with pilots, however.) Actually, personality is a major factor for its pilots, too. I remember getting into some turbulence on a Southwest Airlines flight and hearing the captain suddenly singing a parody of the *Gilligan's Island* theme song over the intercom: "The weather started getting rough, Flight 605 was tossed. If not for the courage of the fearless crew (he then named himself and his co-pilot)..." Everyone on the plane laughed, and the fears were eased. One Target store manager told me that he hired for the three Fs: fast, fun and friendly. He learned that if people were fast, fun and friendly, he could train them in virtually any retailing skill.

If you do the first two force multipliers well, finding and retaining good folks will be a lot easier. The Mirage Hotel has a long waiting list of people wanting to be on their housekeeping team, because friends tell friends what its like to work in a positive environment. Disney has no shortage of applicants who want to work for a place that makes people happy.

Nevertheless, you must have a good hiring process in place that separates the wheat from the chaff and delivers people with the right mix of personality, skill and trainability to create a world-class service team. Space does not permit me to delve deeply into this process, but remember that it *must* involve behavior-based interviewing. Be sure you use a battery of interview questions that will reveal a person's personality style, conflict and communication style and overall demeanor toward customer service. In my seminar, I share an interviewing tool that includes questions like these:

- Describe a time to me when you had to deal with a difficult customer (fellow student, teammate). How did you work with this person, and what was the outcome?
- Describe a time when you had a sharp disagreement with a co-worker (teammate, family member), and what you did to resolve the disagreement. How did it turn out?
- Share with me your personal customer service philosophy. How do you intend to live it if you work for us?
- Give me an example of when you went the extra mile in satisfying a customer. What did you do?
- Tell me about a time when you chose to set aside a company policy in order to meet the needs of a customer. How did it turn out?
- Please read our mission statement and tell me in your own words what it means to you and how you would apply it on the job if we hire you.

Note that these kinds of behavior-based questions leave no room for simple "yes" or "no" answers. They will give you a much better feel for how a candidate will perform under pressure by giving you insights into his or her personality and values. Remember that an ounce of prevention is worth a pound of cure. Any leader who has had to go through the process of firing an employee knows this is true.

Now rate your organization on Force Multiplier #3.

Our hiring processes

Tend to result in poor hires and difficult, unmotivated service personnel.	1 2 3 4 5 6 7 8 9 10	Deliver us the right mix of employees for working with our customers.
Our hiring interview questions are based mostly on skills.	1 2 3 4 5 6 7 8 9 10	Our behavior-based questions reveal a person's true personality and values.

Force Multiplier # 4: The Power of Treating Folks Right

Stephen R. Covey has said, *"Always treat your employees exactly the way you'd like them to treat your finest customer."* This powerful statement rings true because of a simple reality: Your internal customers (your staff) will rarely treat the external customer better than they are being treated by the company (or by each other!). I once watched as a store manager belittled and berated a downcast young employee for leaving some part of his job undone. The outright cruelty and the abuse of positional power literally poisoned the air in the room. When I went up to the employee a few minutes later to be served, the glazed-eye look and the sullen resentment were still evident. I saw other customers who felt it as well. What a tragic and tremendous cost to this company!

When our children were very young, about twenty years ago, my wife cross-stitched a piece that is still framed on our wall. It says, "They may not remember what you said, but they will always remember how you made them feel." I also appreciate another query I once saw on a plaque: "When we want someone to do better, why do we make them feel worse?" I know of few truer statements about the reality of human relationships. The way your employees feel about working for you will, in great measure, ultimately determine the experience your customers will have.

The best way to help an employee reach his greatest potential is to leverage his unique strengths, not emphasize his weaknesses. Most employees are doing the right things ninety-five percent of the time yet are harangued over the five percent that they do wrong. Ask yourself: "Would I really like to work here if I were a box boy or a cashier? What does it feel like to be seventeen in this store? Am I valued, wanted and treated like a pearl of great price or treated like a throwaway commodity?"

As a leader, fiercely protect your employees from your own weaknesses and also from the weaknesses of their fellow employees. Some ideas include:

- Insist on, and personally model, that all people are treated with respect and dignity and courtesy.
- Nip backbiting, belittling and insulting behaviors in the bud instantly (and sometimes publicly) to show that such things are non-negotiable.
- At the same time, reward instances when you see employees and managers treating each other well.
- Publish a "Team member's Bill of Rights," and see that it is always enforced. It could include "The right to be respected," "The right to try and fail" and "The right to state your opinion and be valued for doing so."

Now, rate yourself in Force Multiplier #4.

How do we treat each other?

Employees often feel belittled, devalued, disheartened and hurt in our culture.	1 2 3 4 5 6 7 8 9 10	Employees are uplifted, encouraged and heartened by our culture and environment.
Our overall spirit at work is negative and draining. Emphasis is on correcting weaknesses.	1 2 3 4 5 6 7 8 9 10	Our overall spirit is uplifting, positive and enlivening. Our emphasis is on leveraging our strengths and recognizing what we do well.

Force Multiplier # 5: The Power of Building Service Teams

Daniel Webster once said,

> "Men can do jointly what they cannot do singly, and the union of hearts and minds, the concentration of power, becomes almost omnipotent."

Great leaders learn to synergize the unique strengths of individuals into powerful teams. This is critical as you build your service organization. Quite often, we tend to create what I call "functional silos" in our organization: the cashier silo, the stockage silo, the meat department silo, the management silo. People work in their particular silos, oblivious and uncaring about the work done in other silos. This generates the "not my job" syndrome, the "go ask that guy over there" syndrome and the "someone should take care of that customer" syndrome, all of which are unhealthy to your service system.

I heard Stephen R. Covey relate a situation he witnessed in a Ritz Carlton Hotel. A woman was struggling with her luggage at the door, because no bellhop was present. A maintenance man, who was high on a ladder, replacing a light bulb in the ceiling, witnessed the situation, climbed down and carried the woman's luggage through check-in and onto the elevator. Stephen was so impressed, he approached the man, who simply repeated the Ritz Carlton slogan: "I'm a gentleman, serving a lady" and returned to his work. There was no silo there—only a team effort to satisfy the customer.

There is a far cry between work groups and true teams. Work groups consist of individuals who are assigned to occupy a similar time and place. Teams are energetic groups of people who are committed to achieving common objectives, who work well together and enjoy doing so and who produce high-quality results in a united effort. Work groups simply happen, while teams are consciously, deliberately and constantly built.

Like everything else, the devil is in the details when it comes to customer service. A customer can have great service all through the store but be treated rudely by the cashier, and then all is lost. Some research shows that it takes as many as twelve positive experiences to overcome one extremely negative one—that is, if you even get a chance to recover from it. So great service is delivered by teams that can cross-function for each other and know enough about each other's work to serve in at least the basic ways.

There is not enough space in this chapter to cover all the ideas from my team-building seminar, but here are a few suggestions:

- Promote feelings of belonging in the team. Encourage the creation of warm connections among team members.
- Deemphasize positions, power and hierarchies. Create self-directed work teams, but don't fall into the rut of some leaders who carry this too far and abandon their teams.
- Celebrate team accomplishments, not just individual achievements. Remember, you get what you reward, so if you want teamwork, reward teamwork! A friend of mine who manages a fast-food restaurant promised his employees that if they could, as a team, have perfect closings for thirty days running, he would rent a theater for a midnight showing of the newly-released Star Wars movie. His folks were so fired up that they came into work even when they were not scheduled, late at night, to be sure that things were perfect. He then traded the midnight showing with the theater manager for a catered party for the theater employees. Clever, clever!

- Promote feelings of achievement and contribution by recognizing the value of the team's work and focusing them on the mission.
- Engage in frequent team-building activities. Hint: *The Encyclopedia of Team-building Activities* by Jossey-Bass is a great source, and there are others. Great teams do not just happen; they are consciously built.
- When possible, assign projects to be done by teams rather than by individuals, and give the team a challenge to beat a previous record or other mark on the wall. In the Army, we learned to train and fight as teams.

It's time to rate yourself in Force Multiplier #5.

Are we teams or work groups?

People tend to work independently, have personal agendas and compete internally, with little interdependent interaction.	1 2 3 4 5 6 7 8 9 10	People work in united interdependence, compete externally, with shared interaction and a sense of belonging.
We rarely or inconsistently engage in team building and team thinking.	1 2 3 4 5 6 7 8 9 10	We are constantly engaging in team-building activities and promoting team thinking.

Force Multiplier # 6: The Power of Challenging Your Processes

The final force multiplier I will address is absolutely critical. Leaders know that nothing is ever perfect and that all systems can be improved. This does not mean that we engage in change for change's sake. It does mean that we are constantly benchmarking ourselves and stretching to find new and better ways to do business and serve customers.

This has become increasingly critical in recent years. It is now almost impossible to rely on product or price differentiation alone to carve your niche in the market. As soon as a good idea or product is released, competitors soon mirror it. And someone somewhere will sell it cheaper than you, if only on eBay! The way to truly differentiate yourself is with your service strategies. To do this, you must challenge every process, every procedure, every policy to see if there is a better way to do it from the customer's standpoint.

I have witnessed that over time, organizations tend to create procedures and policies that make work easier or more efficient from the employees' standpoint. We also tend to have knee-jerk reactions and write policies to cover every one-percent-unusual situation that arises, not recognizing that we have just created an extra step or frustration for ninety-nine percent of our customers. Soon, our policy and procedures manuals are inches thick, and our customers' frustrations are a mile high.

A great religious leader whom I deeply admire, Joseph Smith, was once asked 160 years ago how he so successfully governed a very disparate group of converts from a dozen nations. He simply said, "I teach them correct principles, and they govern themselves." We can follow this creed in our own leadership at home and at work. Challenge the process, reduce as much as possible into clear principles and release employees to govern themselves accordingly.

To challenge the process successfully, I suggest the following:

- Constantly examine your operation as if you were a customer. Call in as if you were a phone customer. What is your phone system like? Start in the parking lot and examine every minute point of impact where a customer engages your services. What is frustrating? What looks good?
- When you find something wrong, fix it!
- Reward problem solving not problem finding. Do not allow any employee to bring you a problem without at least two possible solutions and a recommendation for which one is better. If you reward problem finding you will soon have a pack of panting "golden retrievers," happily bringing you problems to solve. Send them back for solutions!
- Engage in frequent brainstorming sessions to uncover and solve sticky problems. I recommend posting a "challenge of the week" for employees to mull over from Monday to Friday and then having a fast-moving brainstorm session to find solutions.

- Shop the competition and do research to benchmark what the very best are doing. Never get complacent.
- Be flexible in meeting market demands. As successful as Henry Ford was in his initial vision, he doggedly refused to change his ways when customers became bored with the stock, black Model T automobile. Ford said, "Tell the customers they can have any color they want as long as it's black." Soon, he lost major market shares to GM and others who were offering sportier red and blue coupes.
- And remember, the best way to predict your future is to create it. You will never be the lead dog until you find a product or idea that no one else has thought of. The Sony Walkman is such a story. No customer had ever asked Sony to create a portable cassette player with small headphones to wear while jogging. No customer had even thought such technology was possible. Sony engineers simply created it and thus predicted Sony's future. Soon everyone was demanding Walkmans, and Sony had to open entire factories to build them. Now dozens of manufacturers make them, but customers still ask for the Walkman by name. What is the equivalent of your Sony Walkman? Don't wait for customers to ask for it; build it, and they will come!
- Keep your promises. If you ask for suggestions, follow up on them, and make the changes you promise. Nothing douses the hopes of employees more than empty promises.
- Listen to your customers. Hold customer focus groups like Sony does. Involve all stakeholders in challenging your processes. And don't forget to involve your internal customers as well. Are you having employee focus groups to solve internal and external service problems?

So rate yourself on Force Multiplier #6.

How are we at challenging the process?

We have many cumbersome, archaic and frustrating policies, processes and procedures that choke initiative and frustrate our customers.	1 2 3 4 5 6 7 8 9 10	Our processes, policies and procedures are designed with the customer in mind and facilitate our ability to serve them.
Our leaders and culture tend to support problem identification rather than problem solving. Employees are not empowered to solve problems, and decision making and problem solving are centralized.	1 2 3 4 5 6 7 8 9 10	There is a definite spirit of problem solving throughout our team. We encourage, recognize and reward problem solving at all levels and empower problem solving at all levels.

In Conclusion

In this chapter, we have explored how leadership is, and always will be, the decisive force multiplier in every situation, from battlefields to boardrooms. By unlocking the power of extraordinary leadership, you will release the full potential of your service team to provide the cutting-edge service that will make your organization world class.

One of my favorite quotes on leadership, by John Buchanan, reads,

"The task of leadership is not to create greatness in humanity, but to elicit it, for the greatness is already there."

I challenge you to really believe this, for it is true: There is tremendous, untapped power and potential in the current service team, the current products and the current customer base you now have. By following these six force multipliers, you will release this potential and enjoy unprecedented success.

Remember, however, what Arthur Jones said,

> "All organizations are perfectly aligned to
> have the results they are getting."

Unless we have the courage to change, to lead differently and to challenge the status quo, we will remain exactly where we are.

About The Author

Kevin R. Miller

 Kevin R. Miller's engaging and interactive customer service and leadership programs have delighted individuals and teams internationally for over 20 years. As founder of VisionBound International and Success Academy at Sea, he has worked with Fortune 500 companies such as Boeing, ConocoPhillips, Novell and Toyota, as well as numerous educational and government agencies. His programs provide nuts and bolts tools and ideas that help participants make genuine change. Dr. Stephen R. Covey recently said of Kevin, *"A unique combination of character, competence and enthusiasm has made Kevin an extraordinary teacher."* As a former active duty Army officer, Kevin observed first hand the power of leadership as a "force multiplier" and specializes in helping individuals become extraordinary leaders. Kevin has spent many years assisting companies and organizations in creating powerful, effective customer service programs through his renowned "Customers Only Want Two Things" seminar series. His other topics include Crucial Conversations™, stress and time management, team building, strategic thinking and planning, project management and over a dozen others. He also specializes in combining seminars with incentive travel programs aboard cruises and in resort settings around the world. Kevin is active in the National Speaker's Association and lives with his family in Springville, Utah.

Kevin R. Miller, President
VisionBound, International.
976 S. 2300 E.
Springville, UT 84663
Phone: 801-916-7433
Fax: 801-491-7170
Email: getkevin@jrsmail.com
Website: www.visionbound.com

Chapter Three

Now Hear This:
The Key to Great Customer Relations
Is Excellent Phone Service

Jeannie Davis

Who signs your paycheck?

I recently asked this question at our Telephone Imagery program for the customer service representatives of a New Jersey Fortune 500 company. When I acknowledged the eager-to-respond, hand-held-high participant in the middle of the classroom, he answered, "I don't have a signature on my paycheck. I've got EFT" (Electronic Funds Transfer). My response? A surprised yet professional, "Oh really?" Calling upon the next person for an answer yielded an enthusiastic "Yeah! I've got it, too!" So did all the other respondents.

Much to my dismay, no one had the correct answer. They all believed that their livelihoods were dependent on some mystical individual who put money in their bank accounts at regularly scheduled intervals. Sad, but true.

They truthfully didn't know that the customer signs their paychecks. They had never considered that their own livelihoods and well-being were dependent upon the customers they serve.

Ever thought about the dichotomy of the customer and the service provider?

Many of us have lowered our expectations about the level of service we receive from service providers. We have succumbed to the reality of dealing with impatient, uninformed, rude, inconsiderate, robotic or disinterested people—especially over the telephone.

You don't need to be a retail clerk to know how you want to be treated when you're making a purchase at your local department store, florist or supermarket. You don't need to be a sales professional to know how you want to be treated when you're buying an automobile, procuring professional services or acquiring a new home. And you don't need to be a customer service expert to know how you want to be treated when you're calling for information about a particular product or service, complaining about an incorrect billing statement or inquiring about public services provided by city government.

Consumers pay for services and take their business elsewhere when they are dissatisfied or disrespected. Employers pay workers to offer service, and a superficial willingness to do so results in lost business. Many people take on the role of consumer/customer today yet go to work tomorrow with a "they-don't-pay-me-enough-to-put-up-with-this" customer service attitude. They conveniently forget what it's like to be the customer when they arrive at work.

When I ask audiences, "Whatever happened to common courtesy in business relationships?" people generally shake their heads from side to side, grunt, "I dunno" or shrug their shoulders at the disappearance of a characteristic we once valued. Afterward, I casually say to them, "So that's how you feel when you're the customer. How do you think your customers would answer the same question about the level of service you provide?"

Many companies have implemented quick-response surveys to measure their quality of customer service. Order a product online and you sometimes get a follow-up survey via e-mail. Our experiences with dining out, overnight lodging, automobile repairs, lawn care services and even whole-house carpet cleaning can result in phone calls soliciting quick responses about customer satisfaction. Suggestion boxes and comment cards are offered in many business establishments. Businesses are working to gather input regarding their customers' service experiences in different ways.

However, few telephone customer service measurements solicit an instant response. Seldom, if ever, has a service provider ended a phone call with, "Well, Ms. Davis, how did I do?" or "What do you think about my telephone communication skills?" Sure, zillions of phone calls are "monitored for training purposes or accuracy" on a daily basis. And workers end up unemployed because of their lack of product/service knowledge, professionalism or social skills or their indifference to customers once the monitored tapes are reviewed.

Unless we consistently work toward improving our phone skills, we may be treating some of our customers the same way we don't like being treated. Keep in mind that customer service excellence is measured through the customer's perception—not yours.

Steps to Excellent Phone Service

Only take the following steps if you want to be considered a provider of excellent telephone customer service—and if you want your customers to come back for more.

Be ethical in customer relationships:

If the shoe doesn't fit, don't put on a bedroom slipper just to be more comfortable with the customer relationship. Being ethical justifies your actions rather than behaviors. It acknowledges the gap between what ought to be and what really is. It defines what is negotiable and not, what's acceptable and not. And it permeates throughout an organization like a blood transfusion, giving a renewed spirit of energy and vitality to each person who comes in contact with your customers.

All customers want to be treated fairly, with dignity and respect. They need to know that your corporate ethics are not negotiable. When the customer calls to inquire about a missed delivery date, there's no need to lie. After all, one lie generally leads to another and another, which reflects poorly on the corporate image—and you. When you're the customer, you get a strong inkling about the credibility and integrity of a service provider over the phone. His sincerity magically comes through in his voice. You believe him and you trust that what's being said is truthful.

In larger organizations, however, unethical behavior is generally well disguised; other companies expose themselves through numerous complaints registered with local Better Business Bureaus. Misrepresentation of products, high-pressure sales tactics and targeting of particularly vulnerable consumers is of grave concern. One such example was exposed when the Denver/Boulder Better Business Bureau issued its highest marketplace alert against a local water softener company. In her public communication, Jean Herman, BBB president and CEO, said, "We are extremely concerned that the community be aware of the predatory, aggressive scare tactics of this firm and the very questionable gap between what they pretend to be selling and what people actually receive." Among complaints consumers alleged to the BBB were product misrepresentation, falsifying signatures on loan application documents for product financing and no follow-up on resolutions promised to consumers. A summary review of the BBB's files on this company led them to believe that the firm was targeting elderly persons, lower-income households and families including people with disabilities.

In most customer interactions, the service provider or salesperson is perceived as the "Company." The average customer doesn't shake hands with your board of directors or have a regularly scheduled lunch with the executive management team. They work with you, and you're the person they trust to convey ethical actions on behalf of your organization. When we're the customers, we don't like it when the service provider quotes one price over the phone just to get us in the door, and then we discover upon arrival that the real price is higher. Whatever you said you're going to do, you must do.

Over the phone, the customer is unable to see your facial expression, body language or overall disposition. Yet many characteristics do come across, and most of them are attitude related: vocal tone, friendliness, body language, listening, helpfulness, pleasantness, confidence and responsiveness. When you say, "I'll look into that for you and let you know what I find," be certain that you do. "I'll put the contract in the mail today" should mean you'll do just that. Treating others the way you want to be treated speaks volumes about you and your company.

Your customers want you to treat them with respect; give them more than they expect, and make their experience dealing with you and your company as pleasant as possible.

Promote emotional intelligence (EQ) in the workplace:

Provide motivation, necessary resources, emotional incentives, coaching and training that enable employees to relate well to your customers. Get the workers excited about your goals, and make them feel their own needs and contributions are important. As employees of any organization, we not only need to know our jobs, we need to believe in our management team, in what we're doing and why we're doing it. Yet in a survey of executives, Accountemps found that ninety-two percent of 150 executive respondents said that they used

46

e-mail as a substitute for face-to-face meetings with employees, and sixty-two percent said they used it as a substitute for face-to-face conversations. Would this boost your EQ?

The Gallup Organization has researched the viability of EQ and found that many employees are "actively disengaged." They go to work because they have to, are unproductive and are likely to leave the company at the drop of a hat. About seventy-five to eighty percent of workers are achieving much less and don't feel enthusiastic about their work. The authors of Gallup's book *Follow This Path: How the World's Greatest Organizations Drive Growth by Unleashing Human Potential* share insights about connecting to customers on an emotional level and the impact on employee moral and customer loyalty.

The attitudes people display during customer interaction represent a visual image of an organization's culture and the emotional intelligence of its people. When employees are eager to share the organization's lack of support or communication with customers, the outcome often triggers a chain reaction that negates the best corporate advertising and marketing efforts. This attitude is often conveyed to customers in telephone conversations sounding like this: "I don't know. They never tell us anything." Or "Whatever's going on is very hush-hush. I wouldn't be surprised if they close these doors tomorrow." Or "This company is full of baloney. They don't care about me. All they care about is..."

When you're an individual contributor to the success of any organization, you feel valued and worthy—and your customers know it. Celebrate successes by displaying positive customer feedback on bulletin boards, in newsletters and during staff or team meeting discussions.

Revive your telephone etiquette skills:

Most of us have talked on the telephone since we were toddlers. It's no surprise we don't feel compelled to brush up on our telephone etiquette skills. Yet most of my customers ask me for help in getting their employees back to telephone basics. Customers form a judgment about your company based on contact with a single individual. If your people don't demonstrate good telephone etiquette, they leave a negative impression that can be difficult to overcome.

When you call a service provider, you can quickly ascertain whether the person who answers the phone sounds friendly, warm, inviting, interested, knowledgeable or concerned. A caller doesn't need to see your face to know whether you're smiling or not; people hear you smile over the telephone. Your telephone greeting simulates the nice, firm handshake of a face-to-face interaction. As customers, we can tell whether a service provider is rushed, hurried, nonchalant, cynical or just plain inexperienced. And when we're greeted with a warm, friendly, professional tone, we're eager to get on with the business at hand. Place a small mirror beside the telephone on your desk as a friendly reminder that people hear you smile through the telephone.

We need to put forth a greater effort to make our customers feel valued and appreciated. Nobody likes to be put on hold, yet, according to Markus Allen, publisher of *Momentum Marketing*, seven out of ten people who telephone a business are placed on hold, and eighty-four percent of them typically hang up if there's more than thirty seconds of silence on the line. When we're the customers, this matters a great deal; however, in our role as service provider, we may not realize the importance of promptly answering or returning to a call.

We've all experienced being transferred to another department—or two—or three. When the service provider perceives this as an opportunity to introduce you to someone else within her organization, she stays on the line with you until your call is connected, providing a personal escort to the individual or department you're seeking. We could really get excited about not being dumped from one workgroup to another when this liaison gives us the name, department, phone number or extension of the person receiving our call.

In relationship building, being dumped for another person is insult enough. In the business world, being dumped into voice mail a few times a day is enough to send some of us over the edge. Even though we've entered the 21st century, many of us don't like talking to voice messaging systems, let alone playing patty-cake with the many menu options that service providers make available for our convenience. In reality, voice mail isn't the only option. Extending a genuine offer of assistance to the caller can be a more rewarding alternative. Volunteer to help the caller whenever possible, ask if someone else can be of assistance, or take a hand-written message. That ought to knock the caller's socks off!

Present a positive image when callers need to leave you a voice mail message. Even though you're unavailable to receive a call personally, you still need to convey a professional image. Call yourself up! Listen to your recorded voice message. If it doesn't reflect the positive image you want to convey, change it. Put a smile in your voice, speak slowly and clearly, ask for specific information from callers, change recordings when necessary, provide a live-person option, and keep the message simple.

Make time to return phone calls throughout your work day. When we're the customers, we resent not getting return calls in a timely manner. Yet as the service provider, we often forget about putting the shoe on the other foot, taking hours and sometimes days to respond to voice mail messages. I'll bet you've told a few friends about people who haven't returned your calls recently. Whether for personal reasons of disrespect, lack of common courtesy or busyness, someone gets a bad reputation. "Whatever you do, don't bother leaving her a message. She takes forever to get back to you." Or "If I were you, I'd call Chuck. He's really good about returning calls." Sound familiar? Avoid falling into this trap at all costs by returning your calls before the end of the business day. You don't want to be the one getting a bad reputation with your business associates, peers or co-workers.

Utilize these few telephone etiquette scenarios as a start. For more detailed tips, tricks and techniques, read my award-winning book on the subject entitled, *Beyond "Hello": A Practical Guide For Excellent Telephone Communication and Quality Customer Service.*

Demonstrate a "your-problem-is-my-problem" mentality:

Convention has it that the customer is always right. That notion holds true when we're the customers; however, when we become the service provider, this perception is no longer a reality. The customer may not always be right; nevertheless, the customer is still the customer.

For example, take complaint calls, which provide an opportunity for your organization to demonstrate its commitment to customer service excellence across the board. Contrary to popular belief, your customers don't lie awake at night dreaming of something to complain about before calling you the next day. And none of us retrieve the Yellow Pages, put on a blindfold, flip through the pages and randomly choose an unsuspecting service provider to call about our dissatisfaction with their product or service. Generally, something is unsatisfactory, unacceptable, unexplained or just plain doesn't meet the customer's expectations. At least that's what the customer thinks. Yet the manner in which some calls are handled produces less-than-desirable outcomes.

Does your customer service attitude reflect a top-down, corporate philosophy? When your organization sees complaint calls as profit opportunities, it means that:

- Employees know about your products and service.
- They demonstrate a rational, commonsensical temperament in interpersonal relationships.
- They are equipped with all necessary resources to resolve problems in a timely, efficient and satisfactory manner.
- They don't fear reprisal or repercussions for escalating the problem to the decision-making executive ranks.
- They are good listeners.
- They understand and believe in your corporate policy regarding customer service.
- They are empowered.
- They are committed to your corporate mission, value and vision statements.

Most business people know it takes less time, patience, energy and money to maintain a current customer than it takes to seek a new one. When your organization consistently receives complaints about the same problem, it's time to revamp your internal processes, evaluate product or service quality, consult with product development and make some changes to enhance your marketing and advertising efforts.

But handling complaint calls effectively is not just the responsibility of the customer service representative. Quality customer service starts at the top and incorporates the mindset of an entire organization. Your company needs to have a formal process in place to manage complaint calls, and your employees need to possess the skills to do so effectively.

A participant in one of our workshops shared this scenario: "The best customer service experience I ever had made me angry because the customer service rep fixed the problem and I didn't have a chance to vent my anger." I guess some of us still want to have our cake and eat it, too.

Consider using this six-step process to assure you can handle complaint callers in a thoughtful considerate manner:

Complaint Call Strategy[1]

Step 1: Prepare Yourself
☎ Be knowledgeable about company policy.
☎ Speak in a well-modulated vocal tone.
☎ Don't personalize the caller's complaint.
☎ Commit to the adult behavior style.

Step 2: Listen Up!
☎ Hear what is being said.
☎ Provide productive feedback.
☎ Make note of relevant details.
☎ Lend an empathetic ear.

Step 3: Establish Rapport
☎ State your commitment to service excellence.
☎ Obtain the callers confidence.
☎ Keep an open mind.
☎ Ask questions to clarify key points.

Step 4: Focus on Solutions
☎ Determine what will satisfy the caller.
☎ Use positive language.
☎ Be realistic about the problem.
☎ Agree on a solution.

Step 5: Summarize and Close
☎ Confirm the agreements you reach.
☎ Express mutuality throughout the conversation.
☎ Be specific about next steps.
☎ Consider sending written confirmation.

Step 6: Follow Through
☎ Keep your word.
☎ Document all actions taken.
☎ Keep the customer informed.
☎ Make yourself available for follow-up.

---

[1] Excerpted from *Beyond "Hello": A Practical Guide for Excellent Telephone Communication and Quality Customer Service*, by Jeannie Davis, published by Now Hear This, Inc., Publishing.

Own every customer interaction:

Sometimes, when we're the customers, we feel as though the service provider doesn't care about our business one way or another. "It's not my job." "It's not my department." "I don't know who handles that." Giving customers the run-around will unequivocally lose their respect—and business. It doesn't matter whether you're on the phone with them for thirty seconds or thirty minutes, you're obligated to claim that portion of every customer relationship as your own.

Passing the buck creates a ricochet effect, which undoubtedly will have a negative impact on the customer's perception of you and your organization. Most companies work diligently to keep up with new technology and products, current trends and customer requests for specific products or services. Sometimes, only the product-management, marketing and advertising teams know the details surrounding a new marketing campaign or product deployment. And although intentions are good initially, rapid change in many industries causes some organizations to appear dysfunctional when employees are not kept up to speed on changes in products, policies or procedures. With the advent of the Internet, most customers or prospects already know more about your company, its products, services, territories, cost structures and client base than you might think—even before they ever pick up the phone to call you.

Ed Wyvell, owner of Shipping Boxes, Etc., got excited when Jim, a local phone company technician, told him that the company could now provide high-speed Internet service for everyone in his surrounding area. Having DSL capability would surely add value to Ed's business and minimize customer wait time for information about shipping, carrier rates, delivery dates, destinations, best shipping methods, etc. Eager to be of assistance, Jim suggested that Ed contact Reggie, his boss, a technical manager, who could refer him to the right people in the company.

What happened next will undoubtedly remind you of a similar experience. In his own words, Ed says, "I called Reggie, who referred me to Delores, a sales associate who was unaware that the company had announced the expanded availability of DSL. Delores transferred my call to Richard, another sales associate, whom she thought could be helpful. Unfortunately, Richard said he'd never heard anything about it either. He asked me to hold while he checked. Grateful for the interest and concern Richard displayed, I patiently waited while he investigated. After waiting five minutes for his return, I was instructed by a prerecorded message: 'If you'd like to make a call, please hang up, check the number or dial again.' I'd been disconnected. The phone line was dead. I didn't go away, so they made me go away.

"Not willing to give up, I dialed a toll-free phone number. Dominique answered the call, listened intently to my story and committed to call me back after she got some answers. I was thrilled. I was on the right track now. She sounded like someone who really cared. But I never received a return call. Frustrated and losing patience, I called good ol' Reggie again for help. Willing to go the extra mile, Reggie gave me a direct-dial phone number for his friend and sales associate, Mark. But Mark, I was told, didn't work there anymore—Ashley did. She told me, "That's not my area" and disconnected the call. I again dialed the toll-free phone number and spoke with Butch. I told him my story and asked for some answers. He was very evasive. It was clear to me he had no answers either.

"Finally, it dawned on me. Someone had to have an answer. So I asked Butch, 'Do you think the Public Utilities Commission (PUC) can help me?' Sounding like I'd just lit a firecracker under his seat, Butch said he'd contact his manager to see what she could do to help. The next business day, Cindy called me and said DSL wasn't available in my service area; the 'best she could do' was get me an ISDN line.

"Well, ISDN was an improvement over getting the runaround. However, after hearing the features of the system, I learned it wouldn't meet my needs anyway. I thanked her for her help, hung up the phone and started singing the words of an old nursery rhyme that came to mind: 'Ring around the rosie, a pocket full of posies...'"

A survey published by the Youngstown, Ohio, Better Business Bureau cited "poorly informed salespeople," "sales clerks who say, 'It's not my department'" and "sales clerks who cannot describe how a product works" among the greatest complaints they receive about service in the marketplace. All of these problems will be reflected in the telephone service you and your employees offer your customers.

Your company must utilize all appropriate communication channels to keep employees informed. And you need to take responsibility for reading press releases, interoffice communication and company-issued e-mails, voice mails, broadcast faxes and newsletters. Hold management accountable for helping you be the best you can be. And hold yourself accountable for achieving that goal.

Be consistent in service quality and delivery:

In an ideal world, chain stores, franchises and multi-location businesses demonstrate the same level of service quality and delivery at each outlet. Yet our personal experiences seldom prove this to be true. Most of us prefer a retail store, because the management or sales clerks are nicer, friendlier or more knowledgeable or offer a better selection of products than the same store offers in another part of town. We can be choosy about where we take our car for automobile repairs, which daycare facility our kids attend, which supermarket has the best produce or seafood and even which fast-food restaurants we frequent. All too often, we don't have the same luxury when working with service providers over the telephone.

Recently, I encountered a situation with a company whose software I had successfully installed but then had difficulty operating per instructions. I spent nearly two hours on the telephone with a "customer care expert," who finally informed me that the problem was not theirs—it was either a problem with my phone line or my laptop computer modem. I found both possibilities difficult to accept, so I initiated a game of pin-the-tail-on-the-donkey.

Over an additional two-hour period, I called the customer service hotline twice more, speaking to a different person each time. And each time, the service representative had a different fix on exactly what the problem could be. Finally, I reached Amber, who spent less than ten minutes with me on the phone. She was knowledgeable about the product, admitting she learned most of what she knew through trial and error. Amber simply advised me to add my area code to the calling pattern. Voila! Problem solved.

When we're the service provider, we are perturbed when the customer continuously calls back, hoping they'll get someone different next time—someone who is more knowledgeable, understanding, patient or willing to go the extra mile. After all, such a customer not only adds more phone calls to the queue, he or she prolongs customer hold time and presumably insults our intelligence. When we're the customers, however, we often get lucky using this technique.

Many organizations provide extensive product/service training for workers. Others provide a broad-brush overview and throw employees to the sharks. And although we realize that different employees learn, retain and communicate information in different ways, we need to do everything we can to consistently provide customers with courteous, accurate, timely, realistic information and responses or solutions to their concerns.

On the phone, we're already limited to about forty percent of our ability to effectively communicate a message. It's easy to become anxious, frustrated, angry or tongue-tied with a customer. But remember, your customers will hear these emotions in your voice. When a customer is on the line and you're unable to provide an appropriate response or solution, seek advice and guidance from a manager or supervisor who can. Two of the "customer care experts" in the above example did just that. However, their advice nearly caused me to panic thinking about the alternatives—contacting the local phone company to troubleshoot possible problems on the line or finding a local service provider to repair my laptop computer modem, wondering how soon it could be repaired and how much it would cost.

Your management team needs to be up to speed in all areas of product/service knowledge. They need to be certain all procedure manuals and other relevant resources are updated regularly. They ought to be willing to support your ownership of the customer relationship by taking the call themselves, when necessary, and demonstrating a willingness to go the extra mile for the customer. They need to issue a bulletin to other workers advising the appropriate solution for scenario XYZ and to coach employees on how to handle the situation. Service reps need to be proactive about following through, keeping abreast of the outcome, asking appropriate questions, requesting additional training, making relevant notations and reading corporate advisories or alerts. They might even begin the process of information sharing with peers and co-workers. Whatever the processes adopted by your organization, service quality and delivery ought to be the same across the board.

Some of us are not well suited to working with customers over the phone. We're not eager to learn, retain or convey relevant information in an energetic or conversational tone. We're not patient, understanding or compassionate. We go to work to collect a paycheck, not to go the extra mile. Not surprisingly, many of us don't even like talking on the phone. There's nothing wrong with not knowing everything. The problem arises when we're too proud or unwilling to seek appropriate advice and guidance from those who should know.

Educate your customers:

Education means better customer service *and* better sales. For the former, don't assume your customers are knowledgeable about the internal operation of your business; about how your processes flow; about how interdepartmental communication occurs; and how their compliance with certain requirements can impact the outcome of their situation.

The truth is, they don't have a clue.

Emphasis should be placed on both external and internal customer relations. Your external customers don't like being told what they have to do. They appreciate gaining a better understanding of why they need to do it. Even your internal customers can become difficult to deal with when pressured by critical deadlines, nonresponsiveness, miscommunication or a lack of knowledge about what your workgroup does.

My friend Marsha works as an accountant for a national, multi-location, title insurance company. The company carries out its escrow investments through the corporate headquarters office, and Marsha handles all the investments. She inputs the appropriate amount of interest to each account on a monthly basis. Marsha says, "I used to get a lot of calls from accountants in other branches requesting account balance information. I didn't mind pulling up the information in the computer and was always willing to help. At times, I was unable to get the information from the computer right away, which meant I'd have to call the person back. After a while, I decided to explain to the other branch accountants how to retrieve the same information I was giving them. Now they can get their balances any time they want."

Instead of getting upset or frustrated about the abundance of calls she received from branch accountants, Marsha educated her internal customers, who were glad to learn how to retrieve the information for themselves.

Look for opportunities within your organization to be helpful to teammates, peers and co-workers. Share practical, useful information with others when appropriate. Remember there is no "I" in the word "teamwork."

Generally, your customer doesn't have to do anything, least of all do business with you or your company. Our competitive, free-enterprise system dictates that we can do business with whomever we choose—and so can your customers. Examples:

- Help the customer understand how your internal process for tracking a lost shipment will be more expeditious when the Claim for Damages form is completed in its entirety and submitted in a timely manner.

- Even though the company did send a handbill in last month's statement, take a few moments to explain your new billing procedures to those customers who find it difficult to understand.
- Instead of telling the customer, "You'll have to come to our office and sign for the check," ask them to do it, explain the process and share with them the benefit in doing so.
- Rather than assume "She should know better" or "He's so stupid" or "That's a dumb question," explain why things are the way they are.

As far as sales are concerned, consider how you can utilize your telephone interaction with the customer to up-sell or cross-sell your products or services. Has your company recently released a new product or service you believe would be a value-added upgrade for the customer? Letting her know about it shows your interest and concern about her. Sharing a tidbit or two about a new service that will be available in a few months is great for business, especially when you call the customer again once the service is available. When you, the bank teller, see the customer has thousands of dollars sitting in his checking account, ask if he is aware of investment options your bank provides. Talk through a few ideas with him, volunteer to provide informational brochures, refer him to a banker or investment manager who can offer sound advice. Educating your customers about new products or services can be very rewarding.

Be positive and inclusive:

Negative self-talk frequently occurs while we're conversing with our customers. And since eighty percent of what we say to ourselves is negative, we're challenged to spontaneously turn negative thoughts to more positive, powerful thoughts. Reinforce your positive attitude and rid yourself of negative thoughts by using "I" statements. Ask yourself how can "I" turn the following statements into positive thoughts?

- **"You're really taking up a lot of my time."**
- **"They don't pay me enough to put up with this."**
- **"You want it *when*?"**

Once you overcome negative self-talk, using positive words and phrases while conversing with your customers will occur naturally. Simply stated, your customers don't have a corporate policy manual at their fingertips. How does it make you feel when a service provider tells you what he or she can't do? When I've asked audience participants that question, they respond with "Why can't you?" "What can you do?" or "Who can do it?" Your customers don't want to know what you can't do. They want to know what you can do. What you're willing to do. If you're unable to meet the customer's request, say so. Offer alternatives for achieving a desirable, satisfactory outcome. "I'm unable to do ABC. I can, however, do XYZ" and "Perhaps EDF is a viable alternative" are more positive responses.

Instead of adopting a you're-getting-on-my-nerves attitude, create a sense of mutual reliance with every customer. Think of the number of times the words "you" or "I" are used in daily customer conversation. "You said you wanted it now, and I said I can't do that." Or "I'm looking at my notes, and that's not what you said. You said..."

"You's" and "I's" can often lead to feelings of defensiveness or alienation in customer communication. Make every effort to speak in mutuality, using words of inclusion rather than exclusion (e.g. "together," "let's," "we," "our," "jointly," "us"). "Let's take a look at some other options." Or "We can work through this together." Or "Our objective is to come up with an equitable solution for both of us" can be much better alternatives.

Remember that the customer signs your paycheck. When you treat customers as business partners, you create a greater opportunity to assure loyal, long-term relationships.

Practice good cellular phone etiquette:

More than half of all Americans own a cell phone. They've become as much a part of our lives as our residential telephones. Some of us have even given up our home phones to be mobile at all times. Cellular telephones meet a variety of needs, from staying in touch with clients and keeping track of the kids to calling for help in emergencies. Here are some friendly reminders about cell phone usage:

Turn off the ringer. The dichotomy of the customer and the service provider is also evident when cell phones come into play. And the fancy ringing of someone's cell phone interrupts many a business meeting.

When you're in a meeting, the presenter, facilitator, trainer or keynote speaker is the service provider, and you're the customer. All heads turn to look at the person who is too important to silence his or her cell phone. It frustrates others in attendance and is disrespectful to the speaker.

Most cellular service providers offer voice mail as an optional feature, and some include it in your service package. Unless you're waiting for an important phone call, turn your phone off or use the vibration feature. If you're anticipating receiving a call while in a meeting or training session, take a seat in the back of the room near an exit. When the phone vibrates, step outside to answer the call and remember to silence the phone before reentering the meeting room. Answering your phone in the presence of others and speaking in a loud whisper or a hushed tone is distracting, rude and inconsiderate.

Make certain that the satellite signal is strong. Society dictates that we all work at a faster pace and return calls on the run—between breaks at meetings, while running to the bus or train stop or while driving. One of the most common complaints that administrative support personnel share in our training sessions is how poor voice quality and reception interfere with their ability to effectively take a message from the caller. Call recipients complain about incomplete messages, garbled phone numbers and poor pronunciation of words due to interference in reception.

Finish your call first—and on time. It's not unusual for us to want to finish our phone conversations before transacting the business at hand. Some businesses have signs asking customers to turn off their phones before approaching the service desk. As customers, we resent waiting in line only to face a service provider who is talking on the phone when it's our turn to be helped. Yet as service providers, we get perturbed when the customer before us is conversing on his cell phone.

After waiting in line at our local supermarket, Chuck, my husband, was livid when he finally reached the checkout counter and overheard the customer in front of him saying into her cell phone, "Honey, I'm two dollars short. What shouldn't I get?" While checking my luggage with a very nice Skycap on a recent business trip, he shared his frustration over the passenger who approached his podium while talking on the phone, held up two fingers and expected him to interpret the sign. "I didn't know whether he wanted to check two bags, whether he meant 'Wait until I get off the phone' or whether he was extending the peace or victory sign. I did know that the passengers behind him had planes to catch and that I had a job to do."

Recently, I've noticed signs in retail establishments, banks, doctors' offices, pharmacies and even in Small Claims Court that read:

- **"Please finish your conversation prior to approaching service counter."**
- **"Disconnect your call before approaching counter."**
- **"If you're next in line, hang up!"**

It's not difficult to treat others the way you want to be treated. If you expect expedient service, practice putting the shoe on the other foot and be prepared to transact your business in a timely manner. Get off the phone when it's your turn in line.

Practice safe driving habits. Some state laws ban the use of hand-held mobile telephones while driving. And some employers can incur liability for problems caused by an employee's use of cell phones while driving, if the company provides cellular phones or if cellular phone use is a necessary component of a job (Roberts v. Smith Barney). A Gallup poll reveals that a majority of Americans say using a cell phone while driving is "very dangerous," and thirty-six percent believe that it is "somewhat dangerous." Twelve percent admit that their personal use of cell phones has created a situation in which their driving became "dangerous or unsafe."

Think safety first. Have you seen these bumper stickers?

"Your car isn't a phone booth."
"Drive now...Talk later!"

Drivers who talk on the phone put themselves and others at risk. Here are some tips to keep you safe on the road:

- Be on the alert for others talking on the phone while driving. They may not be paying full attention to the road.
- Drive now and talk later unless you're in an emergency.
- Pull over to the side of the road and engage your hazard lights before placing a call.
- Drive defensively; you're not the only one on the road.
- Use a voice-activated phone, which allows you to dial and talk hands-free.
- Purchase a wireless hands-free accessory, enabling both hands to stay on the steering wheel.

- Keep calls brief and to the point if you must talk on the phone while driving.
- Avoid emotional conversations that may cloud your judgment while on the phone.

Ten practical steps toward better phone skills

1. Be an active listener. If you're doing more than half the talking, you're not listening. The more you learn about your customers, the better you can serve them.

2. Establish a rapport by using the customer's name in conversation. But don't overdo it! Ask for the correct name spelling and write the name phonetically if it is difficult to pronounce.

3. End every customer phone call by confirming that you've answered all questions, offering additional assistance and extending a pleasant "Thank you for..."

4. Demonstrate a corporate commitment for positive, timely resolution of complaint calls. Complaint calls are great profit opportunities.

5. When using your voice messaging system, call yourself up! If your recorded message doesn't reflect a positive attitude, friendly voice and enthusiasm, change it!

6. When leaving a voice mail message, know what you want to accomplish with the call. Record clear, rational and thoughtful information in your message.

7. Speak in a well-modulated, conversational tone. Remember that your voice will project emotions, including anxiety, frustration, irritation, impatience and nonchalance.

8. Ask probing questions from a position of curiosity. This demonstrates your genuine interest and concern for seeking the information required.

9. Change your telephone greeting periodically so you don't sound monotonous, canned or impersonal. You don't have a second chance to make a good first impression.

10. Monitor your rate of speech. Fast talkers are marveled at but not heard! And slow talkers can be perceived as indecisive.

Conclusion:

Remember that dichotomy of the customer and the service provider? As customers, we're quick to judge how others manage telephone communication, but we often don't evaluate our own or our employees' communication skills. Let your memory of how others treat you on the phone serve as a framework for creating a positive image your customers will remember with pleasure. When you put yourself in the role of customer, you understand how learning to use the telephone more effectively will strengthen and enhance your company's customer service and marketing efforts.

You need to make telephone communication synonymous with quality customer service. Dale Carnegie once said, "You can make more friends in two months by becoming interested in other people than you can in two years by trying to get people interested in you." In the 21st century, he might have added that you can garner more loyal customers with courteous, knowledgeable, trained employees who know how to make the most of every phone call than you can with those who don't.

Nearly ninety-five percent of all business communication takes place over the telephone—even in this day of Internet and e-mail. Used with respect, courtesy and intelligence, the telephone remains your most powerful and effective business tool.

About The Author

Jeannie Davis

Jeannie Davis has a unique way of stimulating the thoughts and actions of people as they view themselves through the eyes of each customer. Her workshops, seminars and keynotes empower business owners, managers and employees nationwide to maximize the profit- and image-building power of their #1 business communication tool—their telephone. A professional speaker, trainer and award-winning author, she has worked with numerous Fortune 500 companies and has trained thousands. Program participants recognize her genuine passion for encouraging people to make beneficial behavioral changes—and showing them how to do it. The author of many articles, she also wrote *Beyond "Hello": A Practical Guide for Excellent Telephone Communication and Quality Customer Service*. Her 4-pack audio CD series features her most requested "Telephone Imagery" keynote presentations and basic telephone etiquette program. The diversity of her clients demonstrates the value of powerful telephone skills for great customer relations. Her clients include the U.S. Olympic Committee, Raytheon Systems, Federal Reserve Bank, Blue Cross Blue Shield, Wells Fargo, Carlson Wagonlit Travel, Principal Financial Group, ACT Teleconferencing Services, National Association of Home Builders, International Customer Service Association, and more. She is active in the National Speaker's Association and the Colorado Independent Publishers Association.

Jeannie Davis, President
Now Hear This, Inc.
14571 East Mississippi Avenue #213
Aurora, CO 80012
Tel: 303-337-1991 or 800-784-5525
Fax: 303-337-1966
Email: Jeannie@phoneskills.com
Website: www.phoneskills.com

Chapter Four

Benefiting from Customer Feedback

Morris Taylor

Imagine a clear, cloudless morning. You feel exhilarated as you contemplate the new day. The air is abuzz with the sounds of children playing, lawnmowers gnawing at sunburnt grass and car doors slamming as work-weary neighbors pack up their cars and head off for the weekend. You've chosen to relax by the lake, only a scant fifteen-mile drive away, and you've only one last errand to run—to return a sports jacket to the corner cleaners to have them re-treat a stain they missed when they cleaned and pressed the jacket a week earlier. Cheerfully, you walk into the shop and catch the eye of the attendant.

"Hello," you say amiably. The attendant nods. "I had this jacket cleaned last week," you say, stretching the jacket across the counter and pulling a sales receipt from your wallet. "But you didn't get this stain out. Would you—"

"You have to tell us if there's a major stain," interrupts the attendant. "There's a sign in the window. See?"

You turn to see where he's pointing. There is, indeed, a very small sign taped to the lower corner of the front window. You turn back to the attendant. "Well, okay, there's a very tiny sign in your window that I've never noticed, but I didn't think I had to tell you to take out any stains when you cleaned the jacket. That's why I brought it in—to be cleaned. I assumed you'd see the stain."

"No, ma'am."

You are momentarily surprised by his response but recover quickly "Okay, so can you do this over again?"

"Yes, ma'am, but we'll have to charge you."

"What?"

"That's why we put the sign in the window, ma'am."

"Well, I don't care about your sign," you say, growing agitated. "I paid you to have this cleaned once, and I shouldn't have to pay again!"

At that moment, the manager approaches the counter. "What seems to be the problem?" she asks.

Relieved, you turn to the manager, still clutching your stained jacket. "Hello. I had this jacket cleaned here last week, and you didn't take out this stain. I'd like to have it re-cleaned."

The manager takes the jacket from you and examines the stain. "Hmmm. Did you tell us to take out this stain?"

You take a deep breath. "I didn't think I needed to. I brought the jacket in to have it cleaned."

"There's a sign in the window," hums the manager, not looking up at you. "We would have taken it out if you had told us. Now we have to do the whole thing over again."

"How long have you been coming here?" asked the attendant, starting to sort through a pile of clothes just dropped off by another customer at the counter. "The sign's been in the window as long as I've been here."

Exasperated, you take another deep breath. Suddenly, you aren't feeling quite the same as when you walked in the front door only moments before. "Are you going to clean it again, or are you going to return my money?"

The manager sighs loudly. "Mike, write up a new ticket. Have them clean it again, see? No charge." The manager looks at you and forces an uncomfortable smile. "Will that take care of the problem?"

You have just given your local vendor feedback about their service. At this point, how do you feel?

Why feedback is valuable

As providers of products and services to today's consumer market, it is essential that we know what our customers and potential customers want and need; what they like and dislike; what they value and are willing to pay for as well as what they don't value and won't pay for. All of this and more is available to us if we know how to solicit and, more importantly, receive feedback from our target audience. This sounds elementary, but the fact is that every day we overlook, downplay or simply ignore what our customers and potential customers try to tell us. Primarily through our unconscious behaviors, we inadvertently insult them, behave in a manner that is perceived as condescending or patronizing, and in a myriad number of other ways communicate to them that what they are telling us is invalid, unimportant, petty, or otherwise of little or no consequence to us as service providers. As a result, our customers, at best, simply stop talking to us and, at worst, look for vendors and service providers who will listen to them and treat them as if they matter (because they do) and as if what they have to say is important (because it is)!

What is feedback?

Feedback is the response to an output (in the context of customer service, this refers to a product, service or policy) that tells us the degree to which that output had value to its intended receiver. Feedback, then, can elevate and enhance our efforts to gain and maintain business by:

1.   Helping us to improve.

2.   Creating a shared understanding between us and our current and potential customers.

3.   Providing us with an objective social perspective (i.e., the way we look to the outside world) that is impossible for us to obtain simply through self-assessment.

This is not to imply that all feedback has value or should be heeded. To the contrary, some feedback, if acted upon, can potentially lead us in an entirely wrong direction and prove to be our undoing! But that caveat brings us to the inherent beauty of all feedback, which is that feedback is a *gift*. Like any gift, we should feel fortunate that someone thought enough of us to offer it, but at the same time, it is entirely up to us whether we accept it or not.

In this light, receiving feedback should never be seen as a punitive process; instead, it is a response to what we have done that can potentially help us to do it better the next time. And, of course, the better our products and services, the more customers we will gain and retain.

Myths about feedback

There are a handful of misunderstandings or "myths" that act on us subconsciously and impact our ability to derive the full benefits of feedback.

Myth # 1
All feedback is punitive.

False. This myth probably came about because of the way many of us, as children, sometimes interacted with our parents, teachers, coaches and other authority figures. As we grew older, it was probably perpetuated in the workplace through the manner our inexperienced and poorly trained bosses chose to deliver scathing criticism that they loosely labeled as "feedback." ("Hey, Ned. See me in my office in five minutes; I want to give you a little *feedback!*") The fact is that true feedback is punitive only in the mind of the receiver. When seen in its proper and most valuable perspective, feedback offers the opportunity to improve and is therefore no more punitive than the track coach who points out that we need to run our last few laps a little faster or the image consultant who tells us that the hairstyle we've been wearing for years makes us look older than we really are.

Myth # 2
You have to know someone for a while before
you can give good/fair/honest/valuable
feedback.

False. If a total stranger came up to you on the street and pointed out that you had a length of toilet paper attached to your shoe, would you say, "Hey, you can't give me feedback! You don't even know me!"? Of course not. You would sheepishly thank the person and promptly scurry off to detach the offending ornament! The fact is that even total strangers can give us potentially valuable feedback by providing social perspective. Maybe we don't have a longstanding relationship with them, but they can still offer an individual response to what they are seeing, hearing, feeling or otherwise experiencing, and that response can help us improve.

Myth # 3
Feedback from anyone other than an
"expert" is a waste of time.

False. All feedback has value if you can use it to improve your future performance. The five-year-old child who samples your raw cake batter and informs you that it tastes bitter doesn't need to be a professional baker to know that you accidentally used salt instead of sugar in the mix. *All* feedback is worth assessing before deciding whether it has value or not.

Myth # 4
I know how to receive feedback in a manner
that encourages others to offer it.

If you're like ninety-five percent of the people in today's society, the answer to this one is also **False**. Most of us respond to the people who offer us feedback in a way that essentially communicates, "You don't know what you're talking about" or "You wouldn't say that if you had all the facts" or "You've made me feel bad/useless/incompetent." Unfortunately, all of these responses effectively begin the process of training others *not* to give us feedback!

These myths live in our subconscious minds and negatively influence our perceptions and reactions to feedback. Dispelling them is the first step toward getting the most out of customer feedback.

Common reactions to feedback
Think about times when you've offered feedback to a spouse or co-worker. Too often, they reacted in one of the following manners:

- Defensiveness and counter attacking. ("Hey, I wrote the best report I could. Maybe if the statistics you gave me had been more current, our proposal would have been more persuasive!")

- Feeling victimized. ("You're always putting me down. You're just like everybody else around here.")
- Diminished self-confidence. ("I knew I was going to mess it up! I'm just not cut out for this!")
- Accepting the feedback at face value. ("So you think I should've extended the half-off sale for another two weeks? Okay, next time it'll be twice as long!)
- Blanket rejection by attempting to invalidate the feedback. ("I know I'm late for the third time this week, but are you aware that there's a lot of construction on Route 80 right now?")
- Complete shut down. ("Yeah, fine. Are you finished yet, or do you have more to say?")

All of these reactions are less than optimal, because they prevent the receiver from objectively and fairly considering what is being said, and in so doing, they cut off the possibility for breakthrough to the next performance level. Through these and similar reactions to feedback, we essentially throw away a potentially invaluable gift!

The key to receiving feedback objectively is to believe in ourselves—if not in our present skills, abilities and knowledge, then in our potential to learn and to improve. When our focus is on learning and constant improvement rather than on giving a perfect performance each and every time, feedback is much less threatening, and we're able to take it less personally. With a *learn-and-improve* mindset, we can assess the feedback rationally, take from it the parts that have value to us, and let go of the rest without harmful impact to ourselves or to our relationship with the giver.

When are we most likely to accept feedback?

Of course, we don't always reject feedback. There are times when we like it very much, times when we welcome and even solicit it from those around us. We tend to most readily accept and like the feedback we receive when:

1. It aligns or agrees with our self-perceptions. ("You know, that's exactly what I thought. I *should* have been more forceful with Jim in that meeting!")

2. Accepting it helps us reach our desired outcome. ("So you're saying my content is good, but in order to make the debating

team, I need to brush up on my tone and inflection? Okay, I'll work on it!")

3. When a lot of people give us the same feedback. It's difficult to argue when *everyone* is telling us the same thing. ("You think I come across as arrogant in the staff meetings? Gee, Jane and Frank said the same thing to me last week. I guess there's something to it after all.")

4. When we believe in and trust the feedback giver. ("Gosh, Dad, I've always thought that Katie was just being too lenient with the kids. But you think I'm hard on them, too, huh?")

While it's easier to accept feedback that falls into one of the above categories, some of the most valuable feedback we can receive won't agree with out self-perception, will fly in the face of what we thought our desired outcomes were, will come from a single voice in the crowd or will come from someone we barely know at all. If that sounds a lot like a typical consumer, you've begun to understand why learning to receive feedback in a positive manner makes good business sense!

HOW TO GET THE MOST OUT OF CUSTOMER FEEDBACK

The importance of shared values

So if all feedback is a gift and we should welcome it, that means that it's *all* valuable—right? Not exactly. While it's true that feedback is a gift and we should try to get as much of it as we possibly can, it's important to remember that feedback is really about the giver's belief system. In other words, everyone has an opinion based on his or her life experiences, values, personal likes and dislikes, etc. That opinion may or may not help you to improve based on the definition of "improvement" in *your* belief system. And that's as it should be. After all, you're the boss; if it's your own business, you have the right to define good customer service the way you want to. Ultimately, however, you want your definition and standards to attract and retain as many customers as possible. Which is simply one more way of saying that good, solid feedback is like the proverbial manna from heaven! We should do everything we can to encourage it and to let our customers know that we value it and will take it seriously in striving to meet their expectations.

Barriers to receiving feedback

Even with the best of intentions, however, we don't always hear what our customers are trying to tell us. There are barriers that make it difficult to truly listen and understand what's being communicated. The most common barriers include:

1. "Already listening" - This term refers to a peculiar type of listening that makes it difficult to fully understand the speaker's message because we have strong preconceptions about the speaker or the ideas being presented. We may appear to be attentive, but a little voice inside our heads is talking to us and saying all sorts of distracting things that prevent us from really listening to what the speaker has to say. This internal talk can range from such comments as, "This woman complains at least once a week. Why doesn't she give it a rest?" to "Doesn't he know I tried that idea last year and nearly went bankrupt?"

2. Listening in order to respond - Instead of giving the feedback giver our full attention, we are mentally formulating a response. Although we should be focusing on the speaker's message, instead we're waiting for an opportunity to interrupt and give our response. Variations of this type of listening include listening for flaws that allow us to criticize or dismiss the feedback and listening for why an idea or suggestion won't work.

3. Inattentiveness - We are mentally distracted, daydreaming or otherwise preoccupied with something that keeps us from focusing on the feedback giver.

4. Listening selectively - We are listening but only for the parts of the feedback that will validate our own beliefs. This manner of listening is very comfortable, because it prevents us from having to make any real changes in our attitudes or performance.

5. Either/or thinking - This is a way of thinking that labels the feedback as either black or white, true or false, good or bad, reasonable or unreasonable, etc. There is no consideration given to a possible middle road, compromise or blending of ideas.

In order to benefit from feedback, we must somehow train and condition ourselves to overcome these natural tendencies and to be open and receptive.

The Best Way to Receive Feedback: An Eight-Step Process

Let's say a customer has just given you feedback about the neighborhood bank you manage. Here's what she had to say:

"Whenever I come to your bank, it seems I have to talk to three or four different people to get one question answered. No matter whom I talk to, they say, 'That's not my area. You have to talk to Ms. Smith.' And, of course, Ms. Smith thinks Mr. Jones is more knowledgeable, and on and on it goes. I think your people need better training!"

Now what?

Here is an eight-step process for receiving feedback that addresses all of the major barriers and helps us to mentally and emotionally frame them as tools for improving our future performance.

Step One: Be aware of your mental state.

1. *Listen without judgment to understand the perspective of the person giving the feedback.* Take a moment to objectively consider how your product or service looks through his or her eyes, keeping in mind that they don't have the same "insider's" knowledge about your operation that you do, such as how hard you've worked or the many operational problems that are out of your control.

2. *Suspend your "already listening."* Already listening shuts down our ability to see the possibility in what the feedback is offering. Make a conscious effort to concentrate both *physically*—by stopping what you are doing and giving the feedback giver your full attention—and *mentally*.

3. *Be open and avoid taking a defensive stance.* The best way to avoid giving the impression that we are defensive is to refrain from the natural tendency to explain why our performance or actions were the way they were. While the explanation may be quite reasonable, it doesn't really change the feedback, and, in most instances, *the feedback giver doesn't really care!* Our facial expression, tone of voice and body language should all convey the same message: "I'm open to the possibility that I can improve."

4. *Your mindset should be to learn and improve.* Remember that you want to learn as much as possible to improve your product or services. So what if the customer is telling you that your deliverable is below his expectations? The fact that he is taking the time to offer feedback at all is his way of communicating that he would consider doing business with you in the future if you will just assure them that his input is desired and will be given your serious and sincere consideration.

5. *Don't take it personally.* Remember that even when the customer is highly critical, he isn't really talking about you personally; he's talking about your performance as a vendor.

6. *Focus on the content, not the intent.* Remember that the value is in *what* he has to say, not in *how* he says it. If the feedback is less than positive and the customer is frustrated or upset, it may be delivered in angry or accusatory tones. Consciously separate the emotion from the ideas.

Step Two: Mentally assess the feedback.

The following questions will help you to assess the potential value of the feedback you receive.

1. *Do I get the same or similar feedback from more than one person?* If you asked another objective party about the feedback, would he or she agree? If the answer is *yes*, it's probably valid feedback!

2. *Does the person giving the feedback know a lot about the subject or issue he or she is addressing?* If *yes*, you can definitely learn something from this person!

3. *Do I understand this person's expectations, and is he or she reasonable?* Again, if *yes*, you can learn something.

4. *Do I trust that the person's feedback is objective and not based on unrelated factors?* For example, it's possible that the giver could be having a bad day or is upset about something entirely unrelated to your product or service. However, if you trust that the feedback is objective, this obviously adds greater weight to what she has to say.

It's easy to see the value of assessing the feedback you receive using these questions. But here is an important point that too many service providers fail to grasp: *Even if the answer is "no"* to one or all of the above questions, you owe it to yourself and the future of your business to listen. Why? Because the feedback is coming from a customer, and *customers are the lifeblood of your business!*

Of course that's a cliché, but it happens to be true. Here's another timeworn platitude that's been heard over and over again: "The customer is always right." Actually, this is false, as any experienced businessperson will hasten to tell you. *But* the customer is *always* the customer. He puts money in your pocket, helps pay your bills, says good things about you to other potential customers and, in general, gives you a reason to open your doors for business each day. The worst thing you could do is alienate him or treat his opinions in a condescending or insulting manner.

At this point, you may be saying to yourself, "Yes, but there are a few people I know who are infrequent customers at best, spend very little money, are never satisfied, and wouldn't be much of a loss to me if they never came back!" That's one perspective. But let me ask you this: Do you think this person has friends or family members who could potentially purchase your products or services? Do you imagine that she ever talks to co-workers or industry contacts about vendors and service providers? Can you really afford to have this person say negative things about you or your business?

The bottom line is this: It doesn't cost you much to be courteous, attentive and open-minded, even to the biggest sourpuss in town. Fail to do this and it can, and eventually will, cost you plenty!

This point is probably obvious to most of the people reading this book. The problem is that in today's society, people have different standards of "courtesy," "attentiveness" and "open-mindedness." How can we maximize the chances that we will be perceived this way by the majority of our customers and potential customers and encourage the kind of feedback we can really use to improve our products and services? One of the secrets is in the next step!

Step Three: Acknowledge the giver's concern/point of view using empathy.

This is particularly important when the feedback is negative or the giver is feeling angry or frustrated. When people offer feedback, their biggest need is not for the receiver to agree with them but to *understand* them. All the giver usually wants is to be assured that he or she has been given a fair hearing. When we exercise empathy, we aren't saying that we necessarily agree with the other party, only that we comprehend what has been said, that we are able to see things from another perspective, and that we are sincerely willing to give the new ideas some consideration.

Once the feedback has been offered, re-state it to be sure you heard everything. Then use empathy to convey respect for the giver's point of view and a caring attitude. Statements such as, "I can understand why you feel that way" or "I can certainly see why you would have been frustrated with our service department" go a long way in communicating that you care about the other person's feelings and perspective and are interested in learning how you might do better the next time. Empathy also tends to calm people down when they are emotionally upset, and this prepares them to be more helpful and receptive in the next step of the process.

Step Four: Ask clarifying questions.

Once you've heard the core message in the feedback being offered and have expressed empathy, use questions to help you begin focusing on the future rather than dwelling on the past. The feedback was about your past performance; what you want to do now is move directly into the *action* step of considering potential solutions that will improve your performance the next time. In addition, when done correctly, asking clarifying questions makes the giver feel like a collaborative partner in the effort to improve your products or services.

Clarifying questions are solely intended to ensure that you fully understand what the feedback giver has said and that you are not misinterpreting, making assumptions about, or otherwise misunderstanding the message. To get the most out of your questions, follow these five guidelines:

1. Avoid alienating the customer. Again, remain open, positive and receptive, knowing that what he has to offer could potentially make you even better. Don't get angry, frustrated, raise

your voice or otherwise become emotional. (The wrong way: *"I don't see how the parts you received could have been defective; we individually inspect and package every one of them by hand!"* The right way: *"I'm sorry to hear that the parts you received were defective. Tell me more about the nature of the defects."*)

2. Be sure you know what the giver means. Is there more than one possible interpretation for what he has said? If so, seek clarification before proceeding. (The wrong way: *"So you think we should make the classes fun? Okay. What else?"* The right way: *"So you think we should make the classes fun? Tell me what you mean by 'fun.'"*)

3. Don't listen to *respond*; listen to *understand*. Think about your question before voicing it. Too often, our questions are less about getting clarification because something was unclear and more about defending ourselves. (The wrong way: *"But did you see the sign telling customers to point out unusual stains when they bring their laundry in?"* The right way: *"I'm sorry we missed that stain in your blouse. I think we need to do a better job of reminding our customers to point those out to us. We'll be happy to clean that again, but in the meantime, maybe you have a suggestion for how we might let customers know about this."*)

To help you edit your questions and ensure that they are truly intended to help clarify matters, ask yourself:

- Is there a *hidden agenda* behind my question; i.e., "Am I trying to persuade them to my point of view?"
- Am I trying to *invalidate* the feedback?
- Am I asking a question or trying to *justify* my actions?
- Is there really anything that they've said that I *don't understand?*
- Will asking this question help me improve my performance?

4. Avoid *yes/no* questions; instead, use *open questions*. Open questions create a need for the feedback giver to provide more information than was originally offered. For example, instead of asking, "Do you think we should reduce the number of

prompts in our automated phone system?" you might ask, "What do you think we could do to make our automated phone system more user-friendly?" Open questions usually begin with the words "What," "How," "When" or "Where."

Directives are statements that are similar to open questions in that they solicit additional information. Examples of directives include statements that begin with, "Tell me more about..." or "Please explain your view on..."

Closed questions, on the other hand, call for a brief response and limit the amount of new information you can receive. Questions that can be answered with a simple "yes" or "no" response are examples of closed questions. An example of a closed question would be, "Do you think we should open more checkout lines?" That's not a bad question, but a better question would be, "What do you think we could do to improve your shopping experience?" Rewording a closed question into an open question or a directive ensures that you will get the greatest possible amount of information from your customer.

The other problem with relying on closed questions is that we can unintentionally lead people to say things they don't really mean. For example, imagine I say to a customer visiting my ice cream store, "Would you like chocolate or vanilla ice cream, sir?" (His response: "Vanilla, I think.") "And would you like it in a sugar gone or a traditional cone?" ("Sugar.") "And would you like chocolate or strawberry topping on it?" ("Chocolate".) "Okay, so you'd like vanilla ice cream in a sugar cone with chocolate topping, right?" In actuality, the customer may have wanted butter pecan ice cream in a cup with whipped cream and a cherry, but because of the series of closed questions, he was only given a limited number of choices. So whenever possible, use open questions to gain greater clarification and to ensure that you aren't unintentionally putting words in your customer's mouth.

Finally, don't hesitate to ask for specific examples to help clarify the feedback even more. Remember: You want enough information so you know how to improve the next time. The more specific the examples given, the more helpful the feedback is.

5.   Keep asking questions until you feel confident that you know exactly how your customer thinks you could improve next time.

Step Five: When appropriate, use survey questions to solicit specific suggestions.

Don't hesitate to ask for advice if you think it will add greater clarity to the feedback. Any time you ask for information that wasn't provided up front in the feedback, it's a *survey question*. A survey question is future-based as opposed to clarifying questions that are past-based. Here are some more sample questions that might be used to clarify feedback:

- "What, specifically, did I do that made my presentation effective?"
- "If you were in my shoes, what would you do differently?" (Survey question)
- "You mentioned that the employees on the morning shift are sometimes rude. Tell me more about your experience."
- "I'm not sure I'm clear about what your perception of the problem is. Could you please give me some examples?"
- "Is there anything else you can think of right now that I could do to improve my performance?" (Survey question)

Step Six: Restate what you've heard at the conclusion.

Once you gather as much information as possible, feel confident that you understand the feedback, and have a good idea of what the giver thinks you could do to improve, re-state what you think you heard. This provides one last opportunity for you to be sure you heard the message completely and accurately and that you have enough information to take action should you decide to do so.

Step Seven: Sincerely thank the giver for his feedback and assure him you will consider it.

Step Eight: Determine the appropriate response.

There are several possible actions you can take after receiving feedback. You can:

1. Ignore it.

2. Do what the feedback giver has suggested.

3. Take the giver's ideas into consideration but devise another way (e.g., your own way) to address the concerns.

4. Find a compromise position.

5. Abandon or avoid the issue.

6. Seek additional feedback on the issue from other sources.

None of these possible responses are more appropriate than any of the others. Again, it is entirely up to you. If you have remained open-minded and you truly want to improve your products and services, you will eventually figure out the best action to take. Just remember that feedback is a gift. There's no reason to get upset; whether and how you act on it is entirely up to you!

Should you use numbers to rate?

All of the principles and guidelines above apply whether the feedback is received face to face or in written form. If you choose to solicit written feedback, you may be tempted to employ a rating system using numbers to quantify the feedback (e.g., 1 = Poor, 2 = Below average, 3 = Average, 4 = Good, 5 = Outstanding). In soliciting the kind of feedback that can actually help you to improve your products and services, is it a good idea to use this type of system?

To best answer this question, we need to consider the value of using numbers as a means of measuring our performance. Essentially, using numbers to assess our capacity helps us:

1. To understand our work processes and see how we're progressing.

2. To objectively communicate this information to others.

3. To make objectively measured improvement.

In this type of system, each number on the scale should be assigned an objective, quantifiable meaning to ensure that each rater is using a roughly similar standard. But to be truly actionable, the numbers should be accompanied by conversation that explains the value and subjective meaning behind the numbers. In other words, what constitutes a "5" in one customer's mind may not be the same as in another customer's point of view. Hence, combining a number rating system with a space for comments after each item, or placing follow-up phone calls to respondents, can significantly increase the value of such feedback systems.

Responding to Feedback: Process Review

To summarize, in order to derive the most from customer feed-back, follow this eight-step process:

1. Be aware of your mental state. Examine the feedback. Evaluate it positively. Think of feedback as a source of new information to be evaluated objectively.

2. Mentally assess the feedback.

3. Acknowledge the giver's concern. Use empathy!

4. Ask clarifying questions to ensure understanding.

5. Solicit ideas to improve future performance.

6. Restate what you've heard.

7. Thank the giver for her feedback and assure her that it will be considered.

8. Determine the appropriate response.

Let's look again at the scenario that opened this chapter, this time utilizing our process for receiving feedback:

Cheerfully you walk into the local cleaners and catch the eye of the attendant. "Hello," you say amiably.

"Morning," the attendant nods.

"I had this jacket cleaned last week," you say, stretching the jacket across the counter and pulling a sales receipt from your wallet. "But you didn't get this stain out. Would you clean this again?"

The attendant frowns momentarily as he glances down at your jacket. "Oh yes, I remember when you picked this up last week. Gee, this doesn't look good, does it? I'll bet you were pretty frustrated when you got this home."

You nod. "Well, yes. I hated the thought of having to make another trip out here."

At that moment, the manager approaches the counter. "What seems to be the problem?" she asks.

"This lady brought in her jacket last week, and we missed a stain," explains the attendant. The manager takes the jacket from the attendant and examines the stain. The attendant looks at you sheepishly and says to the manager, "I don't think she's very happy right now."

"I don't blame her," says the manager sympathetically as she looks up at you. "I'm sorry we missed that stain. I think we need to do a better job of re-

minding our customers to point things like this out to us. There's a sign in the window, but obviously it's not big enough. We'll be happy to clean that again, at no charge, of course. But in the meantime, maybe you could give us a few suggestions as to how we might do a better job of reminding customers to point this sort of thing out. We don't have to talk now. I'm sure you're in a hurry, but maybe when you pick this up in a day or so, you'll have an idea or two. We'd sure hate to lose good customers over something like this!"

You nod. "Well, you could start by making the sign in the window bigger. I've never even noticed it."

The manager takes a note pad from behind the counter and writes something down. "That's probably a good idea. Anything else?"

"No. Not right now. But I'll let you know."

"Great. And we apologize again. Sorry for the inconvenience."

"No problem," you say as you head out the door, off for a morning at the lake. "These things happen sometimes!"

Once again, you have given your local vendor feedback about their service to you. How do you feel this time?

Closing

At the end of the day, without customer feedback the only way we know how our policies, products and services are being received in the marketplace is by our sales receipts. Ultimately, of course, profits are what keep us in business, but if profits start to decrease, we'll want to know what's wrong so we can correct it or do something different. Conversely, if profits increase, we'll want to know what we're doing right so we can keep doing it. Soliciting feedback and then receiving it in the proper manner will guarantee that everything we need to know in order to meet, and oftentimes exceed, our customers' expectations is only a conversation away!

Morris Taylor

Keynote speaker and training consultant Morris Taylor has been involved in education and training for over 20 years. He has presented over 1,200 lectures, seminars and workshops in a variety of civic and corporate environments including customer service centers, wildlife preserves, amusement parks, and martial arts schools. He has lectured in various countries in Europe, South America, the South Pacific and the Caribbean, as well as throughout the U.S. The development of critical leadership and communication skills is at the core of his presentations and skill-building workshops on customer service, public speaking, negotiation skills, coaching, cultural diversity, and time management. In 2002, Crestcom International, Ltd., rated the #1 management/sales training franchise by Entrepreneur International, Income Opportunities, and Success magazines, hired him to develop and videotape a series of train-the-trainer sessions that are currently in use by its distributors in 49 countries around the world. Several of his recorded lectures on the topics of education, spirituality, and community building are in international distribution, and he is the author of four books, including one to help children cope with death.

Mr. Taylor is owner and President of Talisman Training Associates.

To receive a free subscription to Mr. Taylor's newsletter, The Training Clipboard, send your request to The Clipboard@aol.com with the word "Subscribe" in the subject line.

Morris Taylor
Talisman Training Associates
Round Lake Heights, IL
Phone: 1.888.235.8681
Email: Mtaylor95@aol.com
Web: www.talismantraining.com

Chapter Five

Got Trust? Customers Demand It And Want MORE Of It!

Anne M. Obarski

Customer service is valuable, and developing a customer's trust is priceless. In fact, your customers demand it. The question is: What does trust look like, and are you delivering it?

Have you ever been a "lost customer"? Chances are you have. Most of us have walked out of at least one business, vowing never to return. The reasons can range from employees who are inattentive and products that don't meet our expectations to services that are overpriced, poor merchandise selection and, frequently, a "you're wasting our time" attitude from management.

Can you afford to lose even one customer? Not if you want to be successful. The vital question for your business is whether or not you are meeting your customers' or clients' expectations, every time, every day, without exception.

A lost customer comes with a big price tag. I'll share a personal story to validate how much money could walk out the door with a dissatisfied customer.

I use the services of a dry cleaner weekly. I don't like to iron shirts, so my husband's shirts go to the dry cleaner—light starch, on hangers. Because he wears a suit to work, there is usually a suit or two in the order every other week. My expectations of the dry cleaner are very basic: professionally clean my clothes, have them ready on time and, preferably, remember me when I come in the door.

After a number of years, my dry cleaner was only delivering on one out of three of my expectations. The quality of the service had deteriorated, and their biggest mistake was never remembering my name when I walked through the door. I calculated that I spent an average of $20 a week with this dry cleaner. Not a lot, you say? Well, in just one year, I spent $1,000, and had I chosen to stay with that dry cleaner for ten years, that amount would have soared to $10,000 in dry cleaning. That is precisely what my dry cleaner lost when I chose to go elsewhere!

I also tell others when I receive poor service. That isn't unusual; most people tell about a dozen other people. Statistics show that about one third of the number of people you tell about poor service or broken trust with a company will also choose not to do business with that company.

If four of my friends—who all do a similar amount of business with that dry cleaner—chose not to do business there anymore, the loss could amount to $5,000 in one year, or $50,000 in ten years. That's just from losing five good customers. Multiply one dissatisfied customer—who again tells a dozen more friends—per week, and the numbers can become staggering.

Can you afford even one lost customer?

Trust is built on big moments, and trust is lost through big mistakes. Big moments keep customers coming back; big mistakes drive customers away.

My dry cleaning story is an example of a big mistake! But it is followed by a big moment. I have since found a new dry cleaner! All of this dry cleaner's employees know me by name and acknowledge me every time I come into the store. My husband's shirts are beautifully packaged and perfectly starched. They even have a VIP program for good customers like me! They gave me a special garment bag for my laundry and a key. The key is for the box on the side of the building so that I can drop off my laundry any time of the day or night, whenever it is convenient for me! I even receive a fifteen-percent discount on all of my dry cleaning for being a special customer. Considering how much I spend yearly, I know that will add up. And I bet my friends would like to hear about that kind of savings. Wouldn't you?

To ensure that you'll have more big moments, every employee you hire, every investment you make, every advertisement you run and every product you carry should be centered around the final goal of building trust in your customer's mind. Nothing should ever get in the way of that goal.

Trust is built in a customer's mind when you offer dependable products and services by knowledgeable employees who are efficient and friendly every day. Package trust carefully and professionally deliver it so you will meet and exceed your customers' expectations every day. It is a gift they won't likely want to return. Cement the word "trust" into everything your business does, and your customers won't be complaining to their friends; they will become your cheerleaders for life.

Following are five areas that will help you to package and cement that trust between you and your customer.

Truth

I believe that people want to do business with people who tell the truth. Take a hard look at your mission statement, vision statements and strategic plans. Are they company focused or customer focused? Who benefits first? Do all of your employees know what the company mission and vision statements are, and could they recite them when asked? Furthermore, do they believe that the company stands behind each one of those statements in everything it does?

What about the company advertising? I have seen many ads that say, "Our customers are number one." Number one what? These can be the same companies that keep you in "voice mail jail" or make you wait in line or can't accommodate your schedule when you need to make an appointment. Who's number one then?

> Don't just practice what you preach; preach
> what you practice.

I would imagine that most people would say that when it comes to having your car repaired, it is hard to tell whether the mechanic is telling the truth. Recently, there was a short special on a morning news program about quick oil change businesses. I never really thought about them before, because I have never used them. But I know that occasionally, my husband has.

The program highlighted a big mistake—actually, a huge mistake—on the part of a number of these quick oil change businesses. The special showed how the employees would inform car owners how absolutely filthy their engines were and how they had to have them flushed or it could cause huge problems later. When the car manufacturers were interviewed to get their opinions, the answers were very interesting. They said there should never be a reason to have the engine flushed unless the car's engine is in horrible condition. The only reason that these companies would push that service is to make money off unsuspecting customers (like me!).

They went a step further and took a car into a quick oil change place but did not tell them that the car's oil had *just* been changed. The mechanic got under the car, examined a handful of the fresh oil and said, "Look how filthy this is. You will need a complete oil change and new filter." The expert from the car manufacturer said that was absurd, because all oil *looks* dirty. He agreed that again, this was another ploy to get more business. Big mistake!

So who was telling the truth? I don't think I will be going to a quick oil change place any time soon. The sad part is that customers make assumptions about businesses. I will guarantee that most quick oil change companies are truthful with their clients. But after watching that special, I just don't want to take the chance.

Is there a big moment here? You bet! I have found a great car dealership that takes wonderful care of my car. They follow up with phone calls and post cards and even go as far as washing and vacuuming my car, even when I just take it in for an oil change.

They always inform me of my options when it comes to any type of maintenance that needs to be done, and they never make me feel uncomfortable if I take the lesser of the options in order to meet my budget. They have even given me a rental car on many occasions so I can run errands while they work on my car.

Do you think I believe they tell me the truth? You bet I do. Big moments like that keep customers coming back.

Responsibility

Customers like to do business with companies that believe it is their responsibility to educate their employees and keep them updated. Customers expect it even though they may not always tell you.

You do your employees and your customers a disservice if you don't provide your staff with the tools they need to efficiently and knowledgeably handle your customers' questions. And once is not enough!

Training should be the lifeblood of any successful company, and it should encompass everyone from entry-level positions to the senior management team. Communication, negotiating, dealing with difficult customers, relationship building, life management, organizational and team building skills should be an ongoing part of a business's training program and encompass every employee in the company.

Providing basic job skills training is a given, but adding additional training on intercommunication skills, "soft skills" and life-balance techniques will help to keep your employees working productively as a team, both at work and in their private lives.

I was amazed to find out from a manager of a large nationwide bookstore chain that their training—which used to last two weeks for new hires—has been trimmed to three days. I had to ask myself, "What did they think was so unnecessary that they had to cut it out?" But more importantly, "What was in the original training that they felt every employee should know?"

Customers want to deal with people who are knowledgeable and efficient. A customer's or a client's time is precious to her, and beware if you are the one who is stealing that time from her by making her wait too long to have her important questions answered. Even worse is having employees who do not even have the basic skills to perform their daily duties. Performance-based training should be the core of a businesses training program, and it is highly important to evaluate every employee's performance on an ongoing basis.

I am currently consulting for a small, family-owned grocery store chain. They polled a large number of their current customers to find out what they liked and disliked about the store.

The big moments in the report validated the owners' initial reasons for opening up this special little grocery store years ago: to provide the freshest meats, produce and baked goods while providing a wide variety of items not found in other, large grocery store chains. These positive answers, hands down, indicated that their customers would drive miles to buy their produce and meat items. Customers said, "Your fruit looks like it was hand picked," "Your lunchmeat is so great, I bought it before I went on vacation to our summer cottage" and "Please don't change anything; you are doing a great job!"

However, some of the answers made the store owners cringe. In fact, inquiries into customer dislikes offered different feedback and revealed a few big mistakes. Comments in this area pinpointed some easy-to-solve problems that management may not have even been aware of:

"You don't use the tickets at the meat counter correctly. You don't take them in order, and sometimes you even take people who don't have a ticket. Then when someone makes a comment about that, they complain. What happened to 'the customer is always right'?"

Other comments these very loyal customers made were:

"I am disappointed with some of the employees. When I stand by the counter, the staff ignores me, and sometimes they make me wait until they are ready to help me!"

"I am dissatisfied with the service in the deli. A third of a pound does not mean half a pound, and 'sliced thin' means just that. They just don't seem to listen to what you want. This is why I shop at your store, to get the lunch meat sliced the way I want it!"

"Some of the cashiers make many mistakes and are often curt, impolite and waste time."

It is obvious that their customers will continue to come back—even when they get poor service or deal with inadequately trained sales associates. They want the products this store carries, and they are willing to put up with less-than-perfect service. My question is, "Why should they have to?"

The responsibility of this company is now to match the excellence in product assortment and quality with knowledgeable, well-trained sales associates who offer exemplary customer service—period! Some of these big mistakes could easily be changed into big moments in the customers' minds. However, this needs to be an ongoing process.

Reward employees, and you will see higher performance ratings. Employees will be more loyal to those employers who value their performance. What would it take to develop an on-the-spot rewards program? Such a program works well when a manager is given the ability to reward an excellent job performance on the spot.

To make this program valuable, it is important for a manager to know what motivates each of his employees. A day off during the week may motivate one employee, whereas a gift certificate to a favorite restaurant might motivate another, and maybe the third employee would be thrilled with a crisp twenty-dollar bill in her hand.

> It all goes back to knowing your employees,
> training them, rewarding them and finally
> developing accountability.

I find it amazing when I speak to company executives and ask this simple question: "How often do you sit down and review your people?" I usually get the same answer: "Oh, about once a year, when we give a pay increase." That's not often enough if you run a people-, performance- and profit-driven company that is focused on continued success.

People will perform better at their jobs if they know what they are doing well and what they need to improve upon on an ongoing basis. How quickly would those customers who shop in that grocery store change their minds about the deli employees if the manager quickly addressed the information received on the rating forms? A short meeting with the employees to remind them what a great job they were doing and how being exact every time they weighed lunch-meat for every customer would improve not only their performance but the customers' opinions of the deli department.

On a quarterly basis, sit down with each employee and give him a high five and have a meeting during which you discuss the positive areas of his performance as well as the areas that need a little more work. All of the areas discussed should be directly related to his job performance review sheet, which he knows he will be accountable for at the end of the year. Professionally and positively handle small problems sooner, and you will help improve performance over the long run.

Train, retrain, reward and hold your employees accountable for the performance they give their customers, every day. After all, your customer is telling you it's your responsibility!

Selflessness

People like to do business with companies that are recognizable and are unselfish in how they do business. The longer I live, the more I rely on doing business with people who are established. That's not to say I won't give a new upstart my business, but they just might have to earn it some way first.

I'll explain. Many companies do business because of their name recognition with the public. If I say the word "pineapple," you probably would think of Dole. If I say "coffee shop," you most likely would think of Starbucks. If I say "laundry detergent," you might think of Tide. The list goes on and on when it comes to recognizable product or company names.

I believe that didn't just happen. These companies went to great lengths to become established in the marketplace as leaders. What are you doing to become the recognized leader in your business? When someone mentions that he or she needs a chiropractor, dentist, hairstylist, business consultant, Realtor®, banker, landscaper, etc., is your name the first name people would say? Even better, would someone say, " _____ is the *only* person/company you should call?" That is the ultimate goal.

That type of name recognition doesn't happen overnight. Here are some ways to cement your company's name in your prospect's mind and prove that you are also unselfish in how you do business.

1. What is your focus?

I don't use the word "niche" anymore. I like the word "focus." My logo is a magnifying glass, and I like the idea of obtaining a clearer focus on what is really important.

I grew up in Cleveland, Ohio, in a small corner house that had a huge expanse of sidewalks. I remember occasionally playing with my dad's magnifying glass in the summer, staring at everything from flower petals to bugs to crisp, dry fall leaves. My ornery brother taught me that if, on a hot, late-August day, you set a dry leaf on the sidewalk and angle the magnifying glass at just the right position, you can set the leaf on fire! You had to sit very still, be very patient and be very careful that Mom didn't catch you!

The leaf and magnifying glass lesson has proven to be invaluable when I look at my business. Be focused, be clear, and be patient in everything you do.

That type of clarity is important when it comes to describing what you do in your business. Do you have a thirty-second "commercial" that describes your business? It should be one that you can say when you go to a networking meeting, that makes you memorable and makes people say, "Tell me more."

My thirty-second speech goes something like this: "I am the 'eye' on performance. I work with businesses who want to see themselves through their customers' eyes and with leaders who want more repeat and referral business."

Usually, people will say, "That's interesting. How do you do that?" That opens the door to letting them know that I provide professional speaking, training, consulting, mystery shopping and behavioral assessment tools for businesses that want to take a closer look at their company's performance. It is far better than simply saying, "I am a customer service speaker and consultant." I might as well tell them I do root canals on the side.

My goal is to let satisfied clients become my referral system. I want my clients to remember and repeat some part of that thirty-second commercial. Just like with coffee and Starbucks, I want someone to say, "Customer service? It's Anne M. Obarski and no one else!" Along with that referral, I want them to also say that I am professional and easy to work with.

I recently started to do business with a global company, because the vice president felt that I really cared about their company more than any of the other companies who had bid on the job. My fee was somewhere in the middle, but it was the heart of my business that got me the contract. And might I say that we never met in person? The relationship was established purely over the phone!

2. Who knows what you do?

What organizations do you belong to? How involved are you in the Chamber of Commerce or sponsoring Little League baseball teams? Do you give unselfishly of your time and resources to local charities or to schools in your community?

If I said the word "cheers," you would probably think of that popular TV show "where everybody knows your name." It was a friendly neighborhood bar, where everyone was like family, with all of their quirks and crazy habits. You loved them just the same and probably would not go anywhere else!

Does everyone know your name and what you do? I believe that being successful in business in the future will be hugely dependent upon focusing and developing a large network of repeat and referral business.

In his book *Dig Your Well Before You're Thirsty*, author Harvey McKay says, "If I had to name the single characteristic shared by all the truly successful people I've met over a lifetime, I'd say it is the ability to create and nurture a network of contacts."

For networking to be effective, you must network unselfishly. That is not easy to do. Most people believe that networking means "What can you do for me?" when, if you want to build trust in a client's mind, it should be "What can I do for you?" People like to do business with people who are unselfish.

In my mind, the business icon who best represented unselfishness was Dave Thomas, founder of Wendy's. Dave had four key areas that cemented trust in his customers' minds, which, to me, was the epitome of unselfishness.

I recently found myself on the Dave Thomas home page, where I read the following: "Dave's legacy lives on in his words, his values and in his actions." I clicked on the word "values" and found that Dave had five values by which he lived. There is a powerful message in each one of them.

Value 1—Quality is Our Recipe.

> "When he talked about quality, it wasn't just the food served at Wendy's; it was also the way he treated people and the way he lived his life."

The employees at Wendy's were taught to treat people like family, like someone they would like to see tomorrow!

Value 2—Do the Right Thing.

> "He was a man of his word, and he believed you earn your reputation by the things you do every day. He considered personal integrity the most important value one can have."

Dave Thomas built trust within his company, his employees and the general public who bought his food every day.

Value 3—Treat People with Respect.

> "He lived by the Golden Rule: Treat others the way you would like to be treated. He simplified this by saying, 'Just be nice.' When he met you, he looked you in the eye and remembered your name. He thought that was the greatest sign of respect."

How much could each of us learn from those simple, yet profound points?

Value 4—Profit is Not a Dirty Word.

> "Profit in business means growth and opportunities. It also means being able to share your success with your team and your community."

How do you measure your bottom line?

Value 5—Give Something Back.

> "Dave believed that everyone has a responsibility to give back—to help those who can't help themselves. It means giving of your time and your special skills."

This may have been the biggest secret to his success.

Dave Thomas is a person I would have wanted to meet. I think I probably would have wanted to give him a hug—you know, like family. As he said, "From the very beginning, I never thought of myself as anybody special. And whatever I've accomplished through my life, when I look in the mirror, I still see myself as a hamburger cook." (From *Dave's Way*, 1991)

Unselfish acts of kindness cement *big moments* in the customer's mind. On the other hand, Enron, Martha Stewart, K-Mart, MCI Worldcom, etc., are all prime examples of how selfishness can lead to a downfall. Big mistakes! Huge! Do you think customers are taking a closer look at unselfish companies? You bet they are!

Security

People like to do business with companies that stand behind their products, their services and will do so in the best interest of the customer.

Many times, a customer or client becomes dissatisfied after the purchase or delivery of merchandise or services. The entire sales process may run very smoothly, but then something goes wrong with the product or service, and then it is back in the hands of the company to make it right. Unfortunately, this is where some companies decide to stand on their policies versus what is best for the customer and his or her loyalty in the long run.

I think we all have been in situations where we have had to stand up for what we believed in to finally get a company to see our problems through our eyes. A business acquaintance of mine had a situation with a furniture company that sells a well-known brand of recliners. She purchased a chair for her husband, but near the end of the first year, the fabric started to show an unusual amount of wear.

Her husband was not a big man and did not treat the chair roughly. In fact, he was the only person to use the chair. My acquaintance felt that the company should be notified of the problem, and because they were very well known, she assumed they would offer a number of options for dealing with the problem to her satisfaction.

Like all of us who are busy, it took a while for this task to get to the top of her to-do list. When she finally did call the company, they informed her that her contract on the chair had expired just two days prior. Dozens of phone calls to every manager at every level offered her the same solution: "Sorry. It's your problem now. There's nothing we can or will do about it."

Usually, the word "can't" means "won't," and no one was willing to even take a look at the fabric to see what the precise problem was. Nor did they ask *her* what *she* would like them to do about it! Big mistake!

Here was a customer who had the finances to buy anywhere, and she bought at this store because of its history. She said she will never buy anything ever again at that store, and she is on a mission to tell everyone she knows about her experience.

When making a purchase, people need to feel comfortable that the company will stand behind its product or services. Do I think the customer is always right? No. But the customer is always the customer. They buy your cars, pay for your vacations, and they can dismiss you if you upset them. So while it is important to understand and enforce company policy, there also comes a point when common sense should override paperwork. The Ritz Carlton, for example, gives its employees full decision-making power when there is any problem, and they are allowed to use their best judgment to solve it, always keeping the customer's best interest in mind.

What type of security do you offer to your customers? Is it a money-back guarantee, a replacement of the product or sometimes going way beyond what the original contract stated in order to completely satisfy the client?

I remember an old sales training adage that said simply, "The sale begins after the sale." Security in the customer's mind is a way of rating the products, performance and people of your company. Big moments in the area of security occur when a company delivers on that performance in such a way that the customer never forgets and becomes a cheerleader for that company.

Prudential Insurance says you can "own a piece of the rock," Sears Craftsman tools are guaranteed for life, and many of us grew up looking for the Good Housekeeping Seal of Approval. These companies evoke the feeling of security.

I am sure you can think of many big moments when a company has stood behind its products and you have been thrilled. It could have been anything from taking back a moldy package of hotdog buns to fixing the recall problem on your car to staying on the phone with you for hours to help you fix a computer problem. It's not the problem that is important in the customer's eyes; it's how you solve it that makes the difference. That's the definition of security!

Teambuilding

People like to do business with companies whose employees all appear to be playing on the same team.

SAS airlines calls them MOTs or Moments of Truth. I take this concept a step further and call it the "customer's report card" for your company. Customers start making a mental report card for your company based on everyone they come in contact with and how each person has either been a help or a hindrance in that process.

Let's say you need to make a doctor's appointment. You call the office and are suddenly put in voice mail jail and have to wade through nine options before you get to the one that says, "If you want to make an appointment, press nine." Grade: D

You get a very cheerful employee in the office who remembers you and asks how your family is and gets you the very first available appointment that will fit your schedule. Grade: A

You arrive at the office ten minutes early for your appointment, but they are running very late, and you wait twenty minutes to get to see the doctor. Grade: C

The nurse greets you warmly and takes you into the examining room and does all of the essential tests with efficiency and even offers you a magazine before she says the wonderful words, "The doctor will see you in a few minutes." Grade: B

The doctor arrives in record time and listens carefully to all of your problems and makes his diagnosis in record time and even leaves a little extra time to talk about your golf game. At the end of your appointment, you mention that the phone system is very aggravating and that you had to wait too long to be seen. His tone changes, and he says, "Sorry. That's how it usually is here!" Grade: B-minus (Now, if you *love* your doctor, you put up with the inconveniences. But isn't it a shame that we usually do?)

You have made a report card in your mind for that doctor, and, based on your past experience, you will have the same level of expectation the next time, which means that it will probably be a C+ performance for the team. This is not necessarily a big mistake for this doctor, because *he* is the one that keeps you coming back, and you are willing to put up with less-than-desirable performances on the parts of the other members of the team.

I remember when my son was little and played on his first soccer team. He was only five and played on the first level of teams called "grasshoppers." The boys were so cute in their little uniforms with shin guards that seemed to cover their whole legs and soccer cleats that they thought really made them run fast!

The coach, as usual, was one of the dads. He would stand on the sidelines and shout strategic plays to these overly excited little soccer players: from getting Mike to stop standing in one place and playing with dandelions to firmly asking Jeffrey not to use his hands on the ball to trying to get everyone running in the same direction. It was like herding cats.

During one of the first games, the coach was trying to yell too many directions to those little players at one time. At that age, the most fun part of the game is just plain running, and that is precisely what one little player did when he got control of the ball. His little legs were running so fast, and the parents were yelling from the sidelines, and he was so excited when he made that final kick and the ball soared into the net. The crowd went wild, and his smile enveloped his whole face!

But just as soon as that smile came, it went just as quickly. You see, the coach and the parents weren't screaming because they were happy; they were furious. It just so happened that he scored the goal into the other team's net! As the coach pulled all of his little players together, he calmly said to the one boy, "Why did you do that?" With big tears in his eyes, the little scorer said, "You never told us which way the goal was!"

How many times do we have unmet expectations of a company or of our own employees, and the simple reason is that someone never taught them the specifics about the goal and how to get there?

I believe that people want to do business with people they trust. As we have seen, trust is made up of: always telling the truth, working unselfishly and responsibly, offering employee and customer security, and achieving your goals by working as team.

Developing that trust is what customers
demand, but they want even MORE of it.

I define MORE as Market Obvious, Repeatable Enthusiasm! If you can build trust in your customers' minds and deliver MORE of it every day, you are building a solid and successful business.

I find it amazing how good business must be for some companies. I am sure you have thought the same thing, either when companies don't call you back when you are asking for information about their product or services or when they treat you like an interruption to their work instead of the very reason for it.

I found that so true recently when we went on a college hunt with my son. It is interesting to see how some things have not changed in thirty years yet how some things are so different.

As we toured those college campuses, one thing that seemed to remain the same was how the buildings still looked prestigious and inviting on the sprawling campuses, with beautiful grassy areas, where you could sit under big shade trees while studying or relaxing. The dorms are still a place to jam as much "stuff" as you can into one small space, and the food, no matter what the selection, is still dorm food! Pizza shops and bars are still a mainstay, and there is something memorable about the smell of the library.

Of course, no campus visit would be complete without the obligatory campus tour and the informational session. As I sat through the first one, I thought to myself, "Okay, let's see how they will sell this university so we will spend almost $100,000 with them."

1. How did they market themselves?

The change I noticed most while college hunting was how they market themselves. The brochures are slick, and the Web sites rival those of Fortune 500 corporations. They bombard prospective students with postcards and follow-up phone calls and e-mails. They act as if you are the most important person in the world to them and that they can't wait for you to be their new "customer."

How do you market yourself to your customers? Do you try a variety of marketing tools and techniques to grab the attention of your prospective customers?

2. How did they show exemplary customer service?

Colleges hire very friendly students to do their tours for prospective families. They are usually upbeat, fresh-faced seniors who know the pulse of the school and are full of answers to any question parents can throw at them. They know how to walk backwards with precision so that they are always facing their prospective customers. They never miss a beat.

I truly enjoyed one tour guide who said, "Remember—there are no stupid questions, just questions that weren't asked!" They respected our time and completed the tours with time to spare.

Are you and your employees upbeat and focused on your customers and prospective clients? Do you "walk your talk" and provide the information that will make your customers' decisions easy ones? Are you respectful of their time, and are you efficient in your presentations?

3. Was there consistency of service?

Since we were visiting large campuses, there were always other tours going on at the same time. You would see them at different stops along the way. It was easy to pick them out. The parents usually had determined looks on their faces, and they had fresh-faced sons or daughters walking a couple of steps to the side. (It is funny how old these kids look as a seniors in high school and how young they look on college campuses.)

As I watched the other tour guides, I was looking for similar presentation skills. I wasn't disappointed. They sported their colleges' T-shirts, big smiles and casual attitudes that put everyone at ease!

Likewise, your employees should not have "a bad day"! Their daily performance is vital to your business. Turn off one customer and you could lose thousands in potential income—not only from them but from those they tell about your company and your service.

4. Does your team show enthusiasm?

We developed a customer report card for each university we visited. We met with no less than a dozen people on each campus. From the person at the visitor's booth, the tour guide, the admissions counselors and the secretaries to the professors, the deans and even the directors of the marching bands, everyone received a grade from us.

Overall, most were eager to answer questions, confirmed their interest in our son and even suggested that we come back again for an additional weekend. Many of their sentences began with, "When you come here..." They wanted our business, asked for it and invited us back with enthusiasm! Each university did its job so well that it will be difficult decision for our son to make.

We gained a level of trust at each school. They each developed a great marketing program; it was obvious how much the employees loved their jobs, showed consistency in service and delivered it with enthusiasm. *Big moment!*

Are you meeting your customers' or clients' expectations, every time, every day, without exception and striving for MORE of it?

Got trust? Your customers demand and deserve MORE of it.

If you want help, help others. If you want trust, trust others. If you want love, give it away. If you want friends, be one. If you want a great team, be a great teammate. That's how it works. -- Dan Zadra

---

Anne M. Obarski

Anne M. Obarski is the *"Eye"* on **Performance"**. She is an author, professional speaker and retail consultant. For almost two decades, Anne has been the Executive Director of Merchandise Concepts, a Pittsburgh, PA based retail-consulting service. Anne works with companies who are people, performance, and profit focused and helps leaders see their businesses through their customer's eyes. She is known for her educational and motivational approach to handling business owners' two major problems: selling merchandise or services profitably and maintaining repeat and referral customers. Her company's mystery shoppers, better known as "Retail Snoops", have secretly "snooped" over 2000 stores searching for excellence in customer service. Her topics include customer service, sales, communication skills, and image. She is Past President of the National Speakers Association—Pittsburgh, PA Chapter, and active in the National Speakers Association since 1996, and sits on the board of a number of non-profit associations.

Anne M. Obarski
Merchandise Concepts
121 Kathy Ann Ct.
McMurray, PA 15317
Tel: 724-941-4149
Fax: 724-941-4304
Email: anne@merchandiseconcepts.com
www.merchandiseconcepts.com

Chapter Six

The Ten Commandments
of Customer Service

John Jay Daly

Foreword

Nothing is more essential to any business or service provider than gaining and maintaining a list of satisfied customers. Some will insist that profits are more important. That is only partially true, for if a business doesn't take superb care of its customers, sooner or later, it won't have any customers; or at least not enough to be profitable. If this happens to your business, you can count on writing a new chapter in your life: Chapter Eleven bankruptcy.

I've spent more than a half century in the demanding world of business—and more than half of that time researching and conducting seminars and workshops on customer care—and I still find it amazing how badly firms of all sizes treat their customers. It's almost as if they think they are doing us a favor by dealing with us.

In addition to having lifelong experience as a customer of goods and services, I also served in public relations positions with three national trade associations—dry cleaners, printers and direct marketers—each with thousands of members. As part of our services, we conducted educational programs to help members deal more effectively with their customers. With this hands-on experience covering more than three decades, I have obviously learned a lot, much of which is being distilled into this chapter.

To further help with this much-needed education, I have developed "Ten Commandments for Customer Caring," which when heeded, comprise a practical, easy-to-use formula for CEOs, managers or anyone who deals with customers. Following these commandments will improve what they do when dealing with those customers.

Reading and heeding doesn't mean that caring for customers will occur automatically, but if someone works hard to understand what each commandment means—and how to implement it—that person's operation is well on the road to having a successful customer-care program.

At end of this foreword, you'll find a list of my Ten Commandments; I suggest that you make a copy that you can either post or circulate among your team. Or if you wish, simply visit my Website— www.johnjaydaly.com—where you will find a copy of these Commandments as well.

Also, at the end of this chapter, you'll find my popular "C-Word Checklist" as an Appendix. I urge serious students to make copies of this list and then think of the various ways they practice those words when dealing with customers. Advanced students might even take the same words, write down their antonyms and notice the ways they deliberately avoid practicing those words. For instance, the opposite of "cordiality" is "indifference" or "hostility." Try thinking of ways how you and your employees can avoid practicing either or both of those attitudes.

Both of these exercises make an excellent in-house training program. Of course, if you wish, I'd be delighted to discuss visiting your workplace to help you get started in caring for customers. Having a superb customer-care program in place and maintaining it at peak efficiency is a neverending, but rewarding, process for top and middle management as well as those in supervisory positions.

Now let's go through my Ten Commandments one by one. Be assured that it is seldom easy to put these commandments into regular practice, and since there are myriad situations to be covered, let's review in outline form what each one really means.

I - Thou shalt treat thy customers—and employees—as thyself.

Everyone knows customers are vitally important, but too few firms recognize that ensuring the satisfaction of each and every employee is essential for dealing with customers. Happy employees can't help but reflect that attitude when dealing with their customers.

This doesn't mean that every day at work is like an employee picnic, but there are some laboring in the customer service vineyard who contend that "customers come second." This startling phrase should jolt managers and supervisors into realizing that those who deal directly with the public can often make or break a firm's reputation. And they can do so with just a few words, an attitude and, of course, with actions or inactions.

I like to fill my workshops with many real-life stories and true anecdotes. One of my more memorable stories took place at a crowded Manhattan restaurant. After my consulting client and I had patiently given our order to our harried waitress (whom I will call "Mildred"), she stormed off, muttering, "Why does everyone come here for lunch?" Those seven words epitomize what is wrong with the attitudes of many employees.

Lest she wreak vengeance on our meal in some subtle way, I waited until we were departing before I called Mildred aside to quietly remind her, "When customers stop coming in for lunch or dinner, guess whose services won't be needed?" One doesn't have to be a rocket scientist to figure that one out, but her seven words summarize why employees need to be reminded of the important roles they play.

To fulfill my first commandment, it's essential that you put into place some sort of training program, however brief, that ensures employees fulfill your firm's goals and objectives, which should be known by every person on the payroll.

Even more important than the training process is the hiring process. Successful firms long ago found that it's easier to hire employees who, for whatever reason, are intrinsically customer-oriented than to instill that vital trait through training alone. Sure, it can be done, and it is, but be cautious about your hiring process. Examine how you evaluate candidates since a superbly talented person who can't stand people should not be in a position to deal with them.

If you reread my first commandment, you might be surprised to realize that some customers don't want to be treated as you would want to be treated. Within reason, it's better to treat them the way *they* want to be treated. Depending on the level of service they are paying for, what they want may be impossible to achieve. But in many cases, it doesn't cost more to (a) find out exactly what they want and (b) within reason, provide it for them.

II - Thou shalt recognize that all thy customers are vitally important, for from them good things flow.

Here's a question that most managers and owners don't answer very well: "How much do you really know about your major (or minor) customers?" Sure, you might know their names and whether they are regulars or occasional customers or first-timers, but you should know much, much more. In today's Information Age, it's easy to gain and retain this information, provided that this is one of your basic customer-care objectives.

Do you know how long your customers have been dealing with you or what their major preferences are? Within the limits of business privacy, has your sales team explored ways that you might be able to obtain more business from your customers, their fellow workers, their friends or their relatives? If you offer a range of programs or services, are you sure your best customers know about additional services you provide? Or do they just use a few? Have you developed in a meaningful and useful way that all-important database? What steps are in place to ensure it's accurately maintained in a timely manner? Do you test regularly to determine that what you are doing still needs to be done? And vice versa.

In addition to all of this, do you sincerely thank customers for dealing with you? It could either be on a significant anniversary or placement of a particular purchase. Within the bounds of privacy, perhaps it may be appropriate to remember their birthdays or significant anniversaries. The anniversary of being your customer can even be an occasion worth noting.

These same guidelines apply to your employees. Does each one know what day he or she started work? Do you have a foolproof way to recognize this and congratulate them in a sincere way? And considering the final phrase of this commandment, do your employees recognize how important customers really are? It goes without saying that employees who have done outstanding work should be recognized by management in a meaningful, tangible way. The sooner and more publicly it's done, the better.

III - Thou shalt regularly determine what thy customers are thinking.

There are many ways to find out if the needs of your customers are being met. This can range from formal surveys—by mail, e-mail or Website—to informal surveys conducted by telephone or in a face-to-face setting. As a business owner, you don't even have to handle this task yourself. Often, such surveys are conducted by third-party firms such as ours.

However you choose to conduct your research, the basic thrust of this commandment is that owners and managers must ensure that their businesses are always sensitive to their customers' needs. Sure, someone like Ali Kaskici, the general manager of the Peninsula Beverly Hills Hotel may say something clever like, "Waiting for customers to tell you what they need is like driving your car by looking in the rearview mirror." Nevertheless, maintaining a varied dialogue with your customers can ensure that you're staying one step ahead of what they need. The bar for better customer service is raised regularly, so what was good enough last year is hardly satisfactory today.

Treat complaints as if they were made of gold. Management studies all agree that most people don't bother to complain; hence, each complaint you get could be multiplied by a factor of from five to ten. By treating them seriously and analyzing the exact nature—type, timing, location, etc.—you may be able to detect a pattern of imminent failure.

Talking with customers during the transaction is useful, but be aware that this is an anecdotal method and not necessarily a statistically valid one. If you can afford it, one of the most effective information-gathering techniques, particularly for high-ticket items, involves systematically telephoning your customers within forty-eight hours of their purchase. Having the right person do this is essential, but you'll likely be surprised at what you find out. Many customers don't like to confront top management and would rather discontinue buying. But if they are telephoned shortly after the purchase, they are more likely to provide information you'll likely not get any other way.

You can also send survey letters with reply devices (such as postcards), and the proliferation of e-mail makes that method worth experimenting with, particularly since it's easy for respondents to reply. Be sure to design your subject line so the message is not dismissed as "Spam." Most important, if you have a Website designed to handle customer feedback, be absolutely sure that it's simple and foolproof and that it will work with various platforms. Even then, provide a way for the customer to request that you send him a printed feedback form.

Another statistically valid method is to call every Nth customer (perhaps divided into past and present customers) just to find out what they think of the services, products, etc., that you offer. After you analyze the results, be sure to share them—good, bad and ugly— with your key employees and elicit suggestions to improve the operation.

IV - Thou shalt make each transaction so pleasant that satisfied customers will return—and urge others to do likewise.

This is one of the hardest commandments to achieve with regularity. However, with sufficient effort and unflagging dedication, more businesses can achieve this laudable goal.

Just because it's not easy, doesn't mean you should be afraid to try. After all, if management and the entire staff work toward achieving this goal, sometimes a sincere smile or genuinely pleasant demeanor can work wonders—even miracles.

Business owners must never forget that the most powerful form of advertising is word of mouth. It also can be the slowest. But slow can be steady, so what's needed for success is for current customers, however infrequent they may be, to tell their friends, neighbors and colleagues about the pleasant experience they had dealing with you. Never forget, however, that word-of-mouth advertising can also work against you, and that is a mighty powerful way for your business or service to fail.

To make this commandment work, you need to carefully devise a strategic plan that will help you identify the many ways you can make transactions pleasant. Then develop specific tactics to achieve this goal. Exactly how will you try to make transactions pleasant? Be specific, and go into detail. To achieve this will, of course, require excellence in hiring, training and monitoring to ensure that you're not surprised by what happens when these steps are put into practice.

I recall the advice from Lawrence Appley, a former president of the American Management Association, who advised seminar attendees: "Good management isn't what you expect; it's what you inspect." Former president Ronald Reagan put it another way when talking about the Soviets nuclear weapons program: "Trust, but verify."

You need to have guidelines for handling specific tasks and likely occurrences. If it's a dental office, how far ahead should you phone patients to remind them of appointments? If it's a restaurant, should you have a procedure for holding reserved tables at busy times? What should that procedure be? Do you monitor business phone conversations? How often and for how long? If you have a retail operation, how do you handle out-of-stock or back-ordered items?

Remember that in the eye of the customers—and those are the ones who count—each and every one of the steps in the shopping or buying experience can be good or bad. Management is largely responsible for ensuring that all of them are pleasant. Sure, there will be exceptions, but management must work hard and unceasingly to make sure that they are just that—exceptions and not the norm.

I stated at the outset that this is a hard commandment to fulfill, but if the effort is regularly successful, you can bask in the pleasant, warm feeling that you have truly accomplished something. Think about the last dozen buying or shopping experiences you have had. Which ones were pleasant? Why? Which ones were unpleasant? Why? My local ListServe was asked to provide names of a good bank. I submitted the name of the bank I use, but another user killed any chance that this bank would get the business when he stated how difficult he had found it to get access to cash. That one negative complaint was read by hundreds of people. The extent of the damage was incalculable.

The more successful you are over time in fulfilling this commandment, the more successful your business will be. And as the just-cited incident shows, the opposite can also be true. It's inevitable that people will deal with firms that practice excellent customer care.

V - Thou shalt recognize that thy customers may not always be right but that they are seldom all wrong.

The old adage "The customer is always right" is not and can never be strictly true. It is potentially so destructive that it should never blindly be followed. The fact is that a small percentage of customers are just plain wrong, but that doesn't mean you shouldn't treat the vast majority with all the respect they are due. That's why the other nine commandments can come in so handy.

In small businesses, where close, personal, friendly relationships are so essential, the wise manager will quickly spot which clients or customers are a bad fit. If the buyer is abusive and unnecessarily belligerent and doesn't correct his or her ways after being told this behavior is not appropriate, it's far better for long-term employee relations to "fire the customer" than to risk losing valuable, competent help.

Having said that, the wise owner or manager will always seek ways to work with the rare customer who is difficult so it appears that the customer is always right. Having operated a small consulting business in Washington, D.C., since the Ford administration (that's how we measure time in the nation's capital), I've learned from bitter experience that it's easier to avoid taking on difficult clients in the first place.

Having been in the business world more than a half century, I've become a quick study when it comes to people's personalities. For the most part, I can also ask colleagues and others I trust to give me a frank evaluation about a potential client's reputation. If it doesn't match the profile I'm trying to achieve, I simply increase my cost estimate so the account likely won't be unprofitable. And if I'm hired, I've brought it on myself.

VI - Thou shalt keep current with relevant aspects of thy operations.

In our complex society, no one person can know everything about what's happening in any individual business. However, there are certain key success indicators that must be closely monitored in addition to developing and randomly inspecting a system that delegates responsibility for key areas.

The adage that I cited earlier—"Management isn't want what you expect; it's what you inspect."—will become vividly, and sometimes sadly, true when you also adopt the practice of "management by walking around" and do so on an irregular, unannounced basis.

The idea isn't to spy on managers and others in the chain of command but to reinforce on them the neverending, unremitting need to keep alert to what the customers are experiencing. It's better for management to discover a flaw than for customers to do so since, depending on the magnitude of the failure, that may affect how they feel about doing business with you.

Be sure you work with your management team to develop and regularly review the key indicators of which you must be aware. Is there anything you need to know hourly or every few hours? Or is a daily report sufficient? What about weekly, monthly, quarterly reports? Be sure that, over time, these reports don't become so routine they are meaningless. Be alert also that if they become unneeded, you should eliminate them.

Logic should tell you, and time will help you recognize, the cyclical or seasonal nature of certain statistics. You may even want to set up a reporting system that involves "management by exception" so that you only get notified when certain high or low parameters are reached.

One key element is the number and type of customer complaints received. As noted earlier, they should be treated like gold for they may be like canaries in the coal mine—an early tip-off to management that something more serious may be wrong. Smart management sets up a meaningful matrix that helps to analyze where the problems are. It could be in certain divisions, in certain geographic locations or in certain types of products or services.

Before he became "America's Mayor" due to his actions after September 11, 2001, Rudolph Giuliani, with help from Police Superintendent Bratton, devised a plan to reduce crime in Manhattan. In his talk to the Dallas Chamber of Commerce, the mayor explained how he made the captain of each police precinct responsible for the decline of crime in his area. His team developed a matrix to record key details about crimes, such as time of day, type of crime, exact location, etc. Since the current captain would suffer the loss of his cherished post if improvements were not made each month, the responsibility for action was driven into the ranks. This meant that fewer officers would be assigned inside for precinct duty or that daytime patrols would be increased. The result was that crime in Manhattan dropped. It also didn't hurt that the mayor was highly visible and not behind his desk.

VII - Thou shalt extend thyself in an inspired spirit of helpfulness to meet the ever-changing needs of thy customers.

The bar for what constitutes excellent customer service is constantly being raised. So whatever was good enough to keep your customers happy last year or even last month may not be enough today. Continually seek to devise ways to improve the level of service you provide in all of your operations. Work carefully and creatively with your team to determine just what steps you need to take to offer even more. Often, this can be done at little cost, and if it's creative, it sometimes can be accomplished with no extra expenditures.

The basic element is to inspire your team to devise ways each of them can be more helpful. A stimulating, creative brainstorming session, if done with the proper spirit and tone, can bring forth ideas management may never have thought of.

For instance, if a customer tells you she is in a hurry, can you devise ways to meet her at the curb of a retail operation at a specific time in order to complete the transaction (cell phones are marvelous tools for this)? Again, caring persons will often prepare a regular customer's order as soon as she walks through the door.

If a spirit of helpfulness can be instilled, there's no limit to the level of service salespersons can provide. It becomes a challenging game, and those who benefit are the customers. But so do the service providers. After all, if they truly care about offering service, they will want to stay above an ever-rising bar. Never forget that customers' needs continue to change and for all sorts of reasons. The wise firm will stay ahead of the customer and provide those needs seamlessly. Surveys show that asking customers, "Can I help you?" when they enter a store is often a turnoff. It's best if employees can be keenly aware of customer needs and then offer to help meet those needs in specific ways.

Make the topic for your next sales meeting "How can we be more helpful to our customers than we already are?" This question should elicit a litany of answers, particularly if you've alerted your team ahead of time and you expect each person to come to the meeting with at least a half dozen answers. The answers can be big or small, but the totality should be impressive.

VIII - Thou shalt realize that customers are provided better service when you respect thy colleagues and thyself since providing service is everyone's privilege.

Maintaining high employee morale is a goal that demands incredible skill. As desirable it is to achieve, however, it's not always possible. But this doesn't mean that management at all levels should not constantly try. What is essential is to create a workplace atmosphere in which there is a genuine spirit of camaraderie focused on the main goal: serving the best interests of each customer.

How many times have you been immersed in a retail buying situation in which there was a palpable chill in the air? Perhaps, a customer was treated as somewhat of a nuisance, and your presence suddenly interrupted the fighting. Contrast that with what should take place. There's a genuine team spirit, and the workers cooperate with each other to ensure that the needs and desires of each customer are willingly catered to.

Yes, bonuses and picnics and even employee parties will help to some degree to attain this type of camaraderie, but the real key lies in the hiring. It's important to administer some of the many tests that have been developed to filter applicants who have little desire to serve people. Those who do have that desire quickly and innately realize that customer service is a team effort; hence, they adjust so they can get along with colleagues, at least during working hours. The best outcome is to develop friendships that transcend the workplace.

The basic idea is to convey to customers, new and repeat, that they are dealing with a team that wants to provide service to them. Thus, if a customer's basic contact isn't there, the contact's colleague can handle the transaction just as easily.

There are countless ways that this spirit of friendliness and cooperation can be instilled in a creative manner. But again, it starts at the top. You can be firm and disciplined but still be friendly can cooperative.

Another solution: When the first sign of jealousy, vindictiveness or spitefulness rears its ugly head, quickly snuff it out. It's like the man who was asked how he always seemed to remember his wife's birthday and their wedding anniversary. His reply: "By forgetting them once."

IX - When thou art a customer, thou shalt accord just treatment to all vendors.

It's been my observation over the decades that firms that maintain a cordial yet businesslike relationship with their vendors—particularly over an extended period—ultimately provide a high level of service to their customers. It's a mutual relationship that benefits all parties. This doesn't mean they won't entertain creative offers from new vendors, but unless that firm can actually provide a measurable differential that's provable, there often is insufficient reason to make the switch. After all, since there are regular vicissitudes that are bound to occur, it's comforting to know that a long-time vendor will go above and beyond to ensure that the customer is well cared for.

What should not be allowed is blatant discrimination insofar as choosing new or alternate vendors. Buyers, of course, should clearly state the terms of payment beforehand and comply with that understanding or contract.

X - Thou shalt ensure that thy management upholds these commandments and promulgates a clear mission statement with visionary goals.

Believing in these commandments is not enough. All employees need to be fully aware that top management genuinely believes in them and practices each of them to the fullest. It's incumbent upon top management to circulate a memo to that effect, post it prominently in different areas of the workplace and use the commandments as the basis for a mission statement.

But doing this once is clearly not enough. I suggest that management recirculate the original memo at least on an annual basis and make it a part of the welcome packet that each new employee receives upon hiring. It's wise to use them as the basis for continual training and lively discussions. The mission statement that the firm promulgates should be well thought out and continually reviewed to ensure that it is still apt for the current activities.

Every firm should have a mission statement and review it regularly to be sure it is still timely and appropriate. One secret to writing a good mission statement is to be brief yet also complete.

A Dynamic Tool: The "C" Word Checklist

The following list of words can be used to help any organization evaluate and improve their customer service. Simply score your company for each word on a scale of 1 to 10 Use your initial score to target areas for improvement. Visit this checklist every quarter to note progress.

Commitment	_____	Creativity	_____
Complaints	_____	Cooperation	_____
Congeniality	_____	Closeness	_____
Competence	_____	Competition	_____
Courage	_____	Calmness	_____
Caring	_____	Change	_____
Costs	_____	Cases	_____
Courtesy	_____	Communication	_____
Compliments	_____	Compromise	_____
Convenience	_____	Clarity	_____
Completeness	_____	Common Sense	_____
Committees	_____	Charisma	_____
Confidence	_____	Consideration	_____
Conviction	_____	Consulting	_____
Creativity	_____		

About The Author

John Jay Daly, APR, Fellow PRSA

John Jay Daly—as President of Daly Communications of Chevy Chase, MD—is an expert in helping businesses of all sizes care for customers. A veteran, in-demand public speaker, John brings to his audiences more than half a century's varied experience in solving public relations challenges in today's dynamic world. After graduating from Georgetown University where he edited the college paper, John began his career on *The Washington Post,* and for two decades served on the PR staffs of three national trade associations before setting up his own firm in 1976. Two national customer caring programs he conceived in the early '70s are still in operation. In addition to the chapter in this volume, John is also the author of *Mastering Meetings* and *A Communicators Chapbook,* each of which contains my Tipsheets and articles to help businesses and individuals achieve their objectives. John has been a member of the Public Relations Society of America since 1958, is a past president of its larges chapter (in Washington DC) and was named in 1998 to the chapter's Hall of Fame in addition to being Accredited as a Fellow of PRSA in 1974. A member of the National Speakers Association since 1978, he served on its Board of Directors throughout the '80s, founded it National Capital Chapter in '80 and which two decades later named it highest annual award for him. John offers meeting planners a variety of topics and invites them to visit his website (www.johnjaydaly.com) to explore "The Daly Double" programming format which provided two topics for a single travel expense. Married since 1952 to the former Lucille Corbett of Scranton, PA., the couple has raised eight children, each a college graduate exploring their own careers. They have 11 grandchildren.

John Jay Daly
President, Daly Communications
5500 Friendship Boulevard, #1926
Chevy Chase, MD 20815-7272
Phone: (301) 656-2510
Email: speaker@johnjaydaly.com
Web: www.johnjaydaly.com

Chapter Seven

Receiving Good Customer Service Means Asking The Right Questions

Ron Street

The National Association of Realtors® recently released an astonishing statistic: Ninety-three percent of all real estate transactions are completed by only seven percent of Realtors®. Referrals by clients, peers and friends have made it possible for me to be one of that seven percent, because I excel in both traditional skills and Internet expertise (as seen at www.WineCountryEstates.com). My comprehensive professional accreditations allow me to help my customers receive superior customer service. Buying or selling a home is one of the most crucial financial transactions of your life. A well-qualified professional who provides excellent customer service is a must. I will tell you how to identify the attributes of good customer service from the prospective of my profession and help you obtain the best value.

The Old Ways

When I first started in real estate in 1971, I determined that I wanted to be more knowledgeable than the competition, so I took all the real estate courses I could cram into my schedule. I did this thinking that this would separate me from the competition and enable me to give all my customers and clients the best in representation. However, I forgot to study myself as a factor. Back then; my customer service was actually built on a dictatorial model similar to that of Attila the Hun.

Let me give you an example: A customer came to my office and said he wanted a home and a barn with "a country feel," but he preferred to be within walking distance of his work. He also wanted a minimum of three bedrooms on over an acre of land. He was very specific regarding these housing needs and the price range within which he was comfortable. I proceeded to inundate him with every listing that remotely met his criteria and told him to go look to his heart's content. If and when he found the property, I would make an appointment for him to see it. If it were indeed "the" property, I would draft the contract to his advantage. While researching the Multiple Listing Service (MLS), I found an exceptional home with a barn, on two thirds of an acre, about three miles from his work. I escorted my customer through the home. When finished, he said, "This just will not work." I spent several more fruitless weeks showing him property, reminding myself of his guidelines, which I thought I had understood, but I was unable to locate the exact type of property that he said he had to have. There was absolutely no way that I would be able to find a property in his price range that remotely met his needs, as I understood them.

He stopped responding to my calls. Guess what—he had purchased a home from another real estate agent! What did he buy? A duplex on a small lot! I told him he was crazy and should have his head examined. The home with the barn I showed him on two thirds of an acre was one of the very best values in the county. I told him that this was what he should have bought. He put me in my place, saying, "Thank you very much for your time, but I really love the duplex, and it is right across the street from my office." Oops! And this happened because I projected my agenda onto this client and failed to adapt to his needs. What a mistake!

Customer Service Is An Active Partnership

Today, my business practices have evolved considerably, and I have learned that in my business, customer service is an active partnership. What really goes into the creation of a productive broker-client relationship is knowledge and up-to-date credentials plus the ability to proactively interact with the personalities and needs of my clients with positive energy, humor and responsiveness. This combination helps me provide customer satisfaction to a diverse range of clients and obtain the maximum satisfaction for their financial, housing and investment needs. My personal goal of providing world-class customer service brings me repeat business and referral business, because satisfied clients use my services time and time again. When you provide excellent customer service, it ensures that your business will be productive.

This chapter is my opportunity to describe in more detail some of the elements I regard as necessary for success in my business. First, everyone wants a reliable, professional agent when they need to purchase or sell their home or invest in real estate. You may have heard war stories from friends about agents who have taken them to see unsuitable properties outside their location and price criteria. If this happens to you, don't waste time; either restate your criteria or find an agent responsive to your needs. I worked with a couple that had delayed purchasing a home in the San Francisco Bay area for more than a year by not firing an agent who did not listen to them. Meanwhile, prices had increased over seventy thousand dollars for the type of home they desired. So before prices or mortgage rates increase, get the right agent for you.

Finding The Right Agent

How do you find the right agent that will provide you the customer service you deserve? If you have recently worked with an agent who has provided you with valuable services, contacting this agent first is a good option. Quality agents have a large network of peers. For instance, I use my membership in Allen Hainge's CyberStars® because of their careful selection process for choosing member agents. This membership gives me national and international networking capabilities as well as a forum where creative solutions to some of the more challenging financing or purchase strategies can be discussed. Consultation with a network of qualified peers is a valuable tool for professionals in any field and guards against employing strategies that may prove to be more difficult than first envisaged.

The next element is an agent's local expertise. In real estate, this translates into detailed, in-depth knowledge of the area in which the agent works. Many people buying homes, investments or property in Sonoma County, California, where I consult, come from outside the county. These buyers may have no idea where certain local problems exist. Remember that agents also may have recently come from outside the area. I met an agent I worked with in Santa Rosa who is now selling property in Sacramento, ninety miles away. Make sure your agent has been in place long enough to know the local area. For example, there are areas in the county where water wells are notoriously low producers or have poor water quality. I know the lay of the land since I have sold property in this area since the '80s.

An agent who is providing good customer service will ensure that you are aware if the property will provide the kind of environment you want for a home or investment, and he or she will give you the historical potential resale value you may need when you come to sell.

The next element that is invaluable is the agent's attention to detail. Someone once told me to look at a person's car to judge his ability to be orderly and organized. If his car is a mess, he may run his office the same way. Orderliness counts. Realtors® are like the conductors of an orchestra. So when one of the parties to the transaction is pounding on the bass drum, the agent has to keep things in balance. He has to coordinate with the listing agent, the selling agent, the buyer, the seller, the title officer, the construction inspector, the pest inspector, the chimney inspector, the well inspector, the septic inspector, the lender, the underwriters, the lender's subset of affiliates, the relatives, friends and associates of the buyer and seller. All these have the potential to create relationship dynamics that can challenge the most patient. The interaction between all these parties in a real estate transaction may create friction, frustration and failure. It takes a very orderly agent to hold things together and keep the process on track in addition to maintaining the integrity of the transaction and managing all the bumps and scrapes in the process. Experience counts, and so does the ability to stay calm.

Another important factor is time management. A Realtor® who takes on too many clients cannot give them all top-quality attention. Quality goes down, delays occur, or they pass the work onto less experienced associates. Remember that quality and quantity are not always synonymous. Check out the person who will care for your sale. The busy Realtor® is not necessarily the best Realtor®.

As with many other businesses, reputation is a valuable indicator of quality of service. A strategy to establish what kind of reputation an agent has earned with associated professionals is an excellent idea. Title companies in California work with every sale that takes place, and they have firsthand knowledge of agent personalities and those agents who provide timely documentation and follow-up. Call and ask for a senior escrow officer. When you have this person on the phone, ask who does a lot of business with her company and who is the easiest, most competent agent with which to work. Listen also for comments about which agent is a good facilitator and negotiator. The average real estate purchase or sale in California can involve in excess of 100 documents that need to be completed. As I mentioned above, a good agent is organized and timely, which is not an easy task for some agents I have had the misfortune to know. Find an experienced professional who will keep everything progressing smoothly. A top agent can reduce the risk of delays or financial losses and even the loss of your purchase to another buyer!

The Right Approach

A consultative approach is the key to meeting the needs of all the parties to a transaction and maintaining a win-win situation for the benefit of all parties during the course of the purchase or sale. Good consultation skills help to facilitate the balance necessary to handle the myriad objections and conflicts that arise in every transaction.

Another skill of an effective Realtor® is the ability to negotiate. Negotiation involves multiple factors. These include agent-to-agent relationships in addition to relationships with associated professionals. Good interpersonal skills help an agent to assess each situation and strategize accordingly. Once again, local knowledge, reputation, relationships within the community, an awareness of financing criteria and aspects of the properties' physical condition are involved. A good agent also ensures that her customers' rights are primary and makes sure that in the closing transactions, necessary inspections and investigations are given enough time to be done comprehensively before the customers commit to their purchases.

I don't do the job of the mortgage broker, but I do have intimate knowledge of which mortgage brokers and bankers are responsive and which companies put the customer first. I also attempt to match personalities as best I can to make the lending process as easy and pleasant as possible. I want to emphasize that one person's meat is another person's poison. A broker I like may be the broker another agent or customer dislikes. It is not just expertise or knowledge; it is also the chemistry of compatibility. This is why, in all this process, you have to do your own due diligence to find the right match for you. I refer to people whose reputations I know are solid, because their worth reflects on my good judgment.

An agent who understands the art of design is also a great asset. When a seller is preparing to place his home on the market or a buyer is choosing a home that requires a considerable amount of work in order to become the home she would like, an agent who has an eye for design is invaluable. This attribute is also valuable when it comes to seeing the potential in a home that is worn or ugly or when the home requires a large amount of work to become desirable. For sellers, good agents can recommend repairs or cosmetic work that will significantly increase the value of the property. They can also provide the names of craftspeople they know who are reputable and provide quality and value. Many times, agents can suggest simple, imaginative changes that make a home more suitable and improve its utility and value. However, not all agents have the ability to envision how to build character and charisma into a setting. Some use staging companies to create a desirable look for a property, and for expensive homes, this may be a wise, additional cost. Consider the agent's level of taste and ask what kinds of styles she prefers. If she likes Victorian homes and you can't stand them, chances are your ideas of good taste may not mesh.

Provide Added Value

Professionals dedicated to good customer service always apply this concept of providing added value to the services they give their customers. I recommend building extensive networks and knowledge about the businesses of other respected and qualified professionals who offer complementary services to your own. This enhances your ability to provide in-depth customer service to your clientele and also increases the potential of referrals to your business.

The local MLS office is also a good source of information about who is efficient and timely, because the MLS staff interacts with agents when they place listings in the service or require assistance. Agents' responses to the MLS may be indicative of their ability to work with others as well as their work ethic when it comes to timeliness.

To check an agent's ethical reputation, you might call your local Realtors® Association. The association will tell you if an agent has had any ethical complaints made against him. In my state, you may also go to the California Department of Real Estate web site, http://www.dre.ca.gov/, to research any complaints or violations of real estate law by the licensee.

For personal references, attend a meeting of a local organization such as the Rotary Club or other community group. If a member refers someone to you in an enthusiastic manner, you may want to check that person out. You may have found an agent who is truly committed to customer service. The value of personal recommendations holds true for most businesses. Reputation is a valuable guide in the selection process in any professional service.

After doing this research, you will find that some names consistently come up on the business community's radar, either because they are very good or because they are to be avoided at all costs. Obviously, it's a good idea to choose from the top end of the list of agents. This way, you increase your chances of finding someone who conducts his business in a successful, hassle-free way and who may be pleasant to work with on a personal level. Remember, though, that one person's meat is another person's poison. You need to be responsible for doing your own due diligence. One person's dream agent may not suit you.

Key Questions To Ask

The following list of topics is a guide to help you decide the competence and professionalism of an agent when you first meet with him or her.

1. Does the agent ask relevant questions regarding your needs and desires?

2. Does the agent speak to you in real estate jargon or in terms you readily understand?

3. Does the agent have professional designations earned over time, which indicates experience?

4. Does the agent have the respect of his/her clientele, the title company, the lender community and the business community?

5. Does the agent have complaints filed against him/her?

6. What networks does the agent belong to? National Association of Realtors® studies show that eighty-two percent of real estate sales are the result of agent contacts through previous clients, referrals, friends, family and personal contacts. This is probably true in your own profession. If so, then be sure that your customers are aware of the kind of professional contacts you maintain in your industry.

7. Does the agent's office strike you as orderly and functional?

8. A good agent can provide objective information about attractive properties from a variety of informational resources, including the Internet, and they can do this immediately in response to your queries.

When you first interview an agent, think about how she establishes her relationship with you. Is it based on an understanding of your goals, or is it based on what she wants to offer you? And how does she facilitate your communication to her? Is she quickly off and running before you have finished what you want to say, or does she spend time not only listening to you but also asking additional, insightful questions to ensure that she has a full understanding of your goals? When an agent is so sure she knows what you want before you have finished, she is basing her ideas on her own projections of what you want instead of listening to you. This is a red flag, almost guaranteed to waste a lot of your time. If you feel rushed or not listened to in the first meeting, it will not get better. A good listener is normally always going to be a good listener; someone who makes fast assumptions or is impatient will continue to be that way. Treat your first contact as a sample of her behavior and assume that further contacts will have similar characteristics.

Who Will Work With You?

When you interview an agent, always ask with whom you will be working. Will you work only with the agent, or does the agent use assistants, or does she delegate to other agents in her employ? If someone else is involved, it does not matter how good the reputation of the principal agent is; if the assistant is disorganized, untimely and overworked, then your experience may become one of frustration and wasted time. If there is someone else delegated to work with you, then interview that person as well.

Remember that the Realtor® can be the best match in the world, but if he takes three days to return a call or doesn't respond to your e-mail in a timely manner, you can end up receiving poor customer service. I make it my goal to be available on my cell phone so that, unless I am already using the phone or in a meeting, my response time is immediate. Find out what your potential Realtor's® policy is for returning phone calls, e-mails and other correspondence. If the Realtor® does not use a cell phone, then find out who will respond to you and what time frames you can reasonably expect. Once you receive the answers to these questions, do a test run. After the interview, check out his e-mail response times, and also telephone the agent or assistant. This helps to differentiate the hype from the reality. Do you get a prompt, personal response, or are you left forever in voice mail hell? Few agents will tell you that they take hours to return calls and only check their e-mail once a day or even less frequently. And though I find it hard to believe, a significant number of agents have not yet embraced modern technology.

Agent, Broker or Realtor®?

A little extra knowledge: In many states, there is a difference between an agent and a real estate broker. A real estate broker has the professional qualifications to handle transactions independently. An agent has a license that allows that agent to work under the direction of a real estate broker. I have a broker's license and work with RE/MAX, because I don't want the administrative duties of running my own agency. Remember: A Realtor® is a licensed real estate broker, which requires additional education, training and experience. A Realtor® associate works under the management of a Realtor®. Since the term associate is often omitted, it is not always obvious who is an associate and who is a fully-fledged broker. Be sure to learn the status of the person with whom you are working. Be aware: all agents or brokers are not Realtors®. Only members of the National Association that have agreed to abide by a strict code of ethics may use the honor of Realtor®.

Ask The Right Questions

For in-depth knowledge of how a particular agent conducts his business, ask for the names of the five most recent transactions he has closed. Yes, you can do this! Follow up with those customers to see if they liked this agent and felt satisfied with the process they went through. Ask if the title company was efficient. If the answer is no, then enquire further; title companies are dependent on agents' efficient handling of paperwork. In a similar way, local mortgage brokers are another potential source of information. They can tell you if this agent is responsible and timely in the way he does business.

I have discovered that the majority of clients that I have not worked with before have little awareness of the complexity of the documentation that has to be completed in a detailed manner in order for their transactions to be completed on time and within the contract guidelines. Make sure your agent educates you. Understanding how agents' systems and customer service policies function reduces the stress involved in the complex business of buying or selling real estate. If you are aware of the myriad circumstances that can occur during a real estate transaction that may create disappointment, delay and/or cause frustration, then you will be better able to understand the process. An agent who has your needs as his primary concern makes life so much easier for you as well as for all the associated professionals involved.

One of my additional credentials is Certified Residential Specialist (CRS). This designation means that I am an agent who is qualified to help you optimize your transaction by identifying better potential properties, clarifying investment potential and helping you understand tax ramifications. As a CRS, I am able to provide this extra level of customer service to my customers.

It all adds up to one thing: a better outcome for you. Money is important. One aspect of investment, whether it is a primary property, such as a home, or a second property bought for vacation or investment, is the way in which it fits your overall financial goals—especially retirement goals. Your income stream (or lack of it) and the desired quality of your lifestyle are critical to your financial means. To this end, I educate my customer about all the costs involved in their life after transaction (LAT). If you have high LAT costs, then you may regret your purchase. This aspect of buying is one where my experience in the financial services industry really informs my customers and guarantees the quality of the service I am able to offer.

Serious Tax Issues

Many times, when people have not sold a property in a long time, they are not aware of the most current tax laws. For example, there was once a one-time $125,000 homeowner exemption that existed for people ages fifty-five and older; it no longer exists. Others still believe that by buying a more expensive home, they can avoid paying capital gains taxes, and this just isn't true either. Taxes do apply. Some people believe that if they have lived in their home for a very long time and then sell, they can then purchase a smaller, less expensive home without a mortgage and without tax consequences. This is just not true. Current tax rules state that each spouse may take $250,000 tax free from the sale of their personal residence, and then the balance is subject to taxation. Also, in January 2003, the State of California added an additional three-and-one-third-percent withholding tax on the sale of real property. Conveying these hard truths in a compassionate way is an art.

Selling investment properties can also be a source of confusion. Tax laws are very specific as to the disposition and transfer of ownership on investment property. IRS section 1031 allows for real property to be traded for "like-kind" property, but this only defers taxes until there is a final sale. Some investors are surprised when told that they may have a substantial capital gains tax due on the sale of their investment property. Always check with your tax advisor or accountant before selling a major investment asset. By properly structuring a transaction, a well-qualified agent can craft the selling agreement to minimize your tax liability and leave you with more spendable income. This kind of expertise is what contributes to outstanding customer service.

With my experience as a Registered Investment Advisor (RIA) and as a Seniors Real Estate Specialist (SRES), I have special training that allows me to provide answers to issues like those above as well as questions that are most important to senior citizens.

Seniors want to know the best estate-planning strategies that will allow them to live comfortably during their retirement years. They want to plan their estates to minimize inheritance and estate taxes and pass on the majority of their estate assets to their families with minimal costs. Careful planning with competent advisors is extremely important. Sometimes, however, the only asset a retiring customer may own is her home and a very small pension or minimum Social Security benefit. In this kind of scenario, other strategies can be explored to provide adequate housing and income for her retirement years. A reverse mortgage may be the solution to staying in her home and having it generate income. Charitable giving with a lifetime annuity is another strategy, especially if the customers are in good health and anticipate a lengthy retirement. This is just a sample of the available options that a qualified agent can help individuals review before retirement. It's a good idea to hire the best professional you can.

Questions For Seniors

Senior homebuyers typically want answers to these questions:

- What is the property tax structure for the county and state I am considering?
- Are there adequate medical/hospital facilities?
- What will we need to pay for an adequate house?
- What is the cost of living index?
- What is the historical appreciation rate on real estate in the area we are considering?

- Can we reasonably expect to afford a house when we are ready to retire?
- What is available in new or near-new construction?
- Is there a limited growth policy in the area that will affect appreciation?
- Are there anticipated shortages of resources such as water?
- What are the costs of heating, air conditioning and other utilities?
- What is the proximity of entertainment, education, social and other services that I may need?
- What "net" dollars are we likely to receive when we sell?
- What about the pros and cons of trying to own our retirement home free and clear? Should we consider a fifteen-year or a thirty-year mortgage?

A very important element of good customer service is educating your clientele: Never assume that they know what you consider to be everyday knowledge. Make sure clients really know the way your industry works. If you have to use industry jargon to explain an issue to your customers, be sure they are familiar with that jargon, and if not, then translate the information into everyday language they more easily understand. Remember that not all customers will reveal their lack of knowledge, because they don't want to appear ignorant. They may choose to move on to another professional rather than try to understand your communications.

In my industry, there are a variety of credentials and designations that may indicate agents' abilities. One online resource I encourage you to check is the National Association of Realtors® at www.Realtor.com. This site gives you a basic list of information. The first criterion they emphasize is to choose a Realtor® who is member of their organization. All members work according to their code of ethics, and believe me, an ethical Realtor® is a must. And yes, I am a member.

Who's On Your Side?

There is a practical distinction in my industry, of which most people are unaware: the function of the agent who represents the buyer. Buyers are usually under the impression that their agents are representing their interests. Well, they are, but they may not feel obliged to keep elements of what they learn about your intentions confidential. What does this mean? It means that if you say you will put in an offer and that if it is refused, you are quite prepared to pay full price, the agent is not bound by any ethical obligation to keep that knowledge confidential. In fact, by the law of sub agency, the agent is obligated to reveal your intention to the seller.

However, there is a separate category of agent who is not bound by the law of sub agency. These agents have the designation of Accredited Buyer's Representative (ABRs). If you sign up with an ABR, she is ethically and legally obliged to maintain your confidences. She cannot inform the seller or the seller's agent of any material fact that you reveal to her. Now isn't that surprising?

You would be amazed how many people who have bought and sold several houses in their lifetimes are quite unaware that what they tell their agent may not be confidential. In the real world, many agents do respect their buyers' confidences, but it isn't necessarily so. Check out your agent's attitude about sharing information before you commit to a relationship.

Ask a potential agent whom he or she will represent. I cannot emphasize how important this is to you. This is the most basic and fundamental question that you could ask. In the past, the agent who was working with the buyer was actually supposed to be working for the seller through the concept of sub agency. This was typical of the majority of MLS listing contracts, and it is still true today. To avoid being compromised by this kind of conflict, make sure the agent you select is an ABR. Working with an ABR, by definition, will protect all your rights. The written agreement will confirm your ABR's responsibilities to you and your responsibilities to your ABR.

"What's the big deal?" you ask. If you choose to select an agent who does not have the ABR designation, then you take the risk that you may lose your negotiating edge. Whatever you tell your agent, if the agent is not an ABR and there is not a signed buyer's agreement between you, then that agent is obligated to inform the seller of any material fact of which he or she is aware. Make sure the agent you are working with has agreed in writing to represent you as a buyer's agent. That way, you lose none of your rights as a buyer.

One other factor to consider is that an Accredited Buyer's Representative can repeat to you anything the seller's agent says. A Realtor® who is not an ABR cannot divulge information she learns during the consulting process, because this would be considered a violation of the agency relationship.

You would be amazed at the information that has been freely given to me as an ABR that has allowed my customers to gain substantial advantage in the negotiating process. For instance, a listing agent may tell me that the seller has to sell before the home goes into foreclosure. An ABR can divulge such information to you freely, which may affect the offer you would be likely to make. Conversely, a non-ABR Realtor® cannot be this direct, because she would violate her agency with the seller. If you are involved in buying a house yourself, please don't give up your rights as a buyer.

I am one of only seven Accredited Buyer's Representatives in Sonoma County. If you would like more information about this point, go to my web site or call me. The phone number is on the site.

There are probably equivalent factors that are unique to your industry that affect how your customer service will be rated. I believe that customer education is a very important and fundamental element of excellent customer service. I know that in the real estate industry, acting as an ABR has enabled me to obtain substantial value for my clients, because in some instances, even the selling Realtors® forgot this important distinction when they were chatting to me about their listings.

Another point that most people neglect to consider when they choose an agent is the potential that agent has to influence and/or educate you about your financial status and prospects. A home is usually the most expensive purchase someone makes in the course of his whole life. When someone buys a car, he often goes for test-drives and visits all the dealers in the area. When you choose your Realtor®, you need to use the same care that you would use in choosing a car dealership. When you are buying or selling real estate, your Realtor® is often the primary person who helps you determine your buying power—that is, your financial reserves plus your borrowing capacity. Realtors® who have some basic information about your available savings, income and current debt are able to refer you to the best-qualified banks and mortgage companies that can arrange your mortgage. In addition, an experienced Realtor® will give you a number of options on how to best leverage your assets and give you the maximum purchasing power, if that is your objective.

Conclusion

There are thousands of Realtors®, therapists, doctors, dentists and other professionals, and like any other profession, there are board-certified ones, and then there are the rest. Since a home purchase is the most money you will probably ever spend in one transaction, it makes sense to spend it with someone who is well qualified. That's where the agent's experience counts and where the credentials that he has earned are a reflection of his commitment to world-class customer service.

It's reputation, consultation and continued education that sort the sheep from the goats. If you're not getting thoroughly good customer service, you have forgotten that your sale or purchase is worth a check for several thousands of dollars for services rendered. You deserve the best. Put your trust in the best. Get the job done right. Choose someone well qualified, who is known for providing excellent customer service.

Find someone who has additional credentials. Only a very small percentage of agents have special residential sales skills and have enhanced their residential and investment real estate sales knowledge through study, dedication and experience. This commitment to staying informed and up to date is the mark of a true professional. I have made it my business to learn as much as I can about my industry, which is why I currently hold five professional designations from the National Association of Realtors®. This is my commitment to excellence. Additionally, I have more than fourteen years' experience in the financial services industry, managing the assets of high-networth individuals and corporations, a major New York Stock Exchange member and an international bank. Having this background in investment management is a major advantage in my field.

If you intend to move to a new state, remember that good agents have national and international networks. I personally consult the RE/MAX agent network or one of my fellow CyberStars® or agents accredited with ABR, CRS or SRES, and I personally interview them to help my clients receive the best agent match.

These are important steps you need to take to find an agent who will provide you with world-class customer service. If you are unsure of where or how to find a good agent, please contact me at www.WineCountryEstates.com. Last but not least, find an agent who enjoys his work. It is great to work with people who enjoy what they do. If he finds personal satisfaction in his work, chances are his customers will, too. As for me, my work is a joy!

Ron Street

Ron Street, licensed real estate broker, and an Accredited Buyer Representative, is one of the top 7% professional Realtors® in the nation. He is known for his world-class customer service and providing strategic solutions for the real estate needs of his clients. Ron has been a broker since 1972. He is a Member of the Graduate Realtors Institute; a Certified Residential Specialist; a Real Estate Cyber Specialist; and a Seniors Real Estate Specialist. These qualifications indicate his exceptional commitment to professional excellence for his clients as well as associated professionals. Buyers, sellers, escrow officers, mortgage brokers, accountants and attorneys love to work with him. Mr. Street represents buyers or sellers through RE/MAX International. Ron's website: WineCountryEstates.com contributes to his success and he is one of Allen Hainge's CyberStars™, an international organization of 150+ agents who employ technology to implement superior personal service. Ron believes in sharing his expertise and is an adjunct professor at Santa Rosa Junior College where he teaches Real Estate Finance and is a regular speaker on real estate for financial planning classes. He also speaks to national and regional audiences about Real Estate Accumulation and Wealth Transfer Strategies for Professionals.

Ron Street, ABR,CRS,GRI,RECS,SRES
Associate Realtor®
RE/MAX Central Santa Rosa
320 College Avenue, Suite 300
Santa Rosa, CA 95401
(707) 579-1190 Direct
(707) 480-8000 Cell
(707) 579-1190 FAX
Website: WineCountryEstates.com
Email: ron@WineCountryEstates.com

Chapter Eight

You Never Get a Second Chance To Make A First Impression

David Jakielo

In today's business environment, it seems that customer service has taken a back seat to price. We have come to expect and accept lousy service, or no service at all. But that's okay; we rationalize, because we are saving money.

The suburban mega store concept has been slowly but surely making the smaller, customer-friendly neighborhood stores close their doors forever. We seem to be willing to trade service for price and perceived convenience of one-stop shopping.

It's only a matter of time before you will be asking, "What aisle for in vitro fertilization?" And some high school kid will respond, "I don't know. That's not my department" and briskly walk away.

Some of my other favorite responses or actions I have experienced from "customer service" personnel are:

"I don't know. I'm new here."

Two employees don't even acknowledge you
but continue discussing the previous
night's party.

"You'll find that in the blue aisle," an employee says, meaning that's the hair color of
the person working in that aisle.

It seems that with our price-conscious public, companies are not willing to invest in employees who have customer service skills. These skills can be learned, but unless a company provides a training program, employees remain clueless as to how to act or react when it comes to dealing with customers.

I don't understand why this important customer service training isn't part of a general high school education. These are skills that can be utilized forever, in all walks of life. Even though I was deprived of this type of education in high school, I'm sure glad I had to take calculus, because even though I have never used calculus in only been 32 years since high school.

However, it's not all bad news. The good news is that if you or your company decide to resurrect the idea of providing excellent customer service, your cash registers and wallet will be overflowing with the green stuff.

An important concept to keep in mind is that providing excellent customer service isn't enough to be successful in today's marketplace. The buzz term I have been hearing is "customer satisfaction." It is important to understand the difference between the two. They are defined as follows:

Customer service - Providing to the customer what you think is important to the customer.

Customer satisfaction - Providing to the customer what he or she thinks is important.

Given the above definitions, we need to keep in mind that we should always be striving for customer satisfaction. A company cannot be successful if it isn't focused on customer satisfaction. This will make customers want to deal with us in the future, because we are meeting their needs from their perspective, not ours. One other concept to keep in mind before we delve into the how-tos of customer satisfaction is learning how to define who our customers are.

It isn't just the people who buy our products and services; customers encompass a much broader scope. I define a customer as anyone with whom we come in contact. Some examples are:

- Anyone buying or recommending our products or services
- Co-workers
- Management
- Suppliers
- Our families and relatives

It is important to remember that customers aren't just the people who come to spend their money with us but people found internally. Every department is the other department's customer. In other words, everyone and anyone who can add to your or your company's success is a customer.

How employees are treated by management and how employees treat each other will be reflected in how we interact with the customer. You can't take the approach of, "Do what I say; don't do what I do." I've experienced times when a manager has yelled at an employee over some issue or employees are permitted to argue among themselves. If the employee is exposed to an environment where it is okay for his boss to yell at him, or if employees are permitted to yell at each other, they will naturally think it's okay to yell at a customer.

To help avoid this problem, treat everyone as if they are your most important customers. This applies whether they are external or internal to the company.

Now that we have gotten some of the definitions out of the way, let's examine the how-tos of dealing with customers.

First Impressions

I'll begin with the topic of first impressions, because, as the old saying goes, "You will never get a second chance to make a first impression." It is important to keep in mind that a person will make various decisions about your business in the first seven to ten seconds of contact. The impressions are formed by observing both verbal and nonverbal actions.

I'm not saying that this is fair, and I'm sure we all have had the experience of forming an opinion about someone only to be proven wrong after we have had a chance to spend more time with that individual. But unfortunately, when it comes to customers, it is rare that we will get the time to change someone's first opinion of us, because if it isn't a positive experience, she will vote with her feet by going somewhere else. Following are some of the decisions customers make within the first few seconds of contact.

Nonverbal

- Are you dressed appropriately and cleanly?
- What message are you sending via your posture?
- Are you responsive?
- Are you friendly?

Verbal

- Do you have an enthusiastic tone of voice?
- Are you courteous?
- Are you helpful?
- Are you knowledgeable?

Let's examine each of the above individually, in more detail.

Nonverbal Impressions

Are you dressed appropriately and cleanly? To answer this question, you need to keep in mind that you aren't just dressing for yourself but for the customers your serve. There isn't any one way to dress, because what's appropriate for working at a tattoo parlor probably won't work at an upscale department store and visa versa.

I'd like to share with you an experience I had while traveling on business. I was checking into a hotel in a small town outside of Chicago. I approached the registration desk, and the clerk had her back to me. When she turned around, I was astounded by the number of holes she had in her head. The openings weren't limited to the five major orifices that most people have—two ears, two nostrils and a mouth. I lost count, but she had at least eight pairs of earrings in her ears and additional trinkets in her lips and nostrils.

I couldn't believe my eyes. I'd understand if I were checking in for the National Piercing Convention, but I checked the daily meeting marquee board, and they weren't holding any special events at the hotel.

Being the curious individual that I am, I returned to the lobby after I checked into my room to see if I could find the general manager. I wanted to ask why the registration clerk was dressed for a hard rock concert rather than in attire more suitable for a business hotel. Okay, so it wasn't one of the upscale hotel chains, but it was a national chain in the moderate price range.

Upon finding the GM (who, surprisingly, was dressed as I had expected—in a coat and tie, with only five major openings in his head), I asked if he had a dress code for his employees. He replied, "Oh, I can't tell my people how to dress." I asked, "Why not? Who signs their paychecks?" Plus, I related to him that there were two additional hotels within walking distance and that business people may be uncomfortable with the first impression his hotel made, based on his front-desk personnel. To this day, I wonder if, instead of frequent travel miles, they were offering a free piercing of your choice with every two-night stay—not that they had many business people who would stay two consecutive nights.

It is important to remember that you should always dress based upon you customers' expectations. Remember that most of our country's disposable income is controlled by people age forty and older; it is better to dress conservatively instead of following the latest trend. People over forty don't relate well to hair that is a primary color, multiple body piercing or flamboyant tattoos.

The laid back casual look of the '90s is slowing melting away, and businesses are readopting more businesslike attire. Some companies are issuing company shirts in specific colors. This still allows employees to dress in a more relaxed casual manner, but it gives the company a "uniformed" look and the employees a sense of belonging.

What message are you sending via your posture? You don't need to stand at attention like you're in the military, but when you stand up straight; you will come across as being attentive or involved with the customer. A slouchy posture sends the nonverbal message that you are not interested or that you lack confidence. Don't lean against walls or counters, and make sure, if your interaction is in a sitting position, that you sit up straight and lean toward the person with whom you are interacting.

Avoid crossing your arms when talking or listening to a customer. That posture may come across as "I'm not interested" or "You're interrupting me; hurry up, so I can get back to what I was doing."

Another important point relating to posture is how you walk. Have you ever encountered a person coming toward you who walked at about .0001 miles per hour and shuffled his feet? This may be appropriate walking speed for a resident of the Shady Rest Nursing Home but not for a mobile individual in a business. Whether greeting a customer or going to find out an answer for her, you should always walk at a quick pace (not a sprint, unless you're a valet parking cars).

Walking at a faster pace sends a message of confidence and attentiveness. A customer will feel better interacting with someone she perceives as confident and attentive. Plus, when you combine these two traits, it also sends the message that you are knowledgeable.

Lastly, never talk to people with your hands in your pockets. When your hands are in your pockets, you have a tendency to rattle change or jingle your keys, and this can be very annoying or distracting.

How responsive are you? There are many ways customers form opinions about our service level. One very important indicator is how responsive we are to them. How quickly we acknowledge the customer's presences can set the tone for the entire interaction.

For example, let's say you are returning an item to the store because it isn't working properly. You get up in the morning and turn on the new coffee maker you just purchased, and nothing happens. Now you are forced to face the day without your morning coffee. Not only are you inconvenienced by not being able to get your caffeine fix but you also enter into a debate with yourself about whether you should have bought this expensive, upscale model in the first place. So not only are you ridden with guilt about splurging for an expensive, fancy machine, now it doesn't even work.

You pack up the coffee maker in its original box; find the receipt and head back to the store where you purchased the item. You're still lacking your daily caffeine fix, because you forgot your charge cards, and you never carry enough cash to purchase a cup of coffee at the local, upscale, coffee emporium. (Remember when you could get a cup of coffee for less than a day's pay?)

You enter the store after driving through a maze of shopping carts, which are scattered throughout the parking lot. It seems they have been strategically placed to ensure that there isn't a parking spot within a quarter-mile radius of the front door.

Even though there are obstacles in your path, your grit and determination land you at the customer service desk, where two highly motivated individuals are located behind the counter. One has his back toward you, head down, and is looking through a pile of papers on a desk; the other seems to be engaged in a personal phone call, making sure that arrangements have been made for that night's party.

You clear your throat a few times, vying for their attention but to no avail. They continue with what they are doing and ignore you. I wish I could say this is an unusual occurrence, but that would be a lie. Unfortunately, this lack of responsiveness seems to be the norm today rather than the exception.

Attention, all customer service personnel: When a customer approaches, remember that she isn't just the most important thing at that moment; she is the only thing. Stop what you are doing and acknowledge her. If you can't drop everything, then inform her that you'll be with her shortly. Customers should not be looked at as an interruption; they are the reason we have our positions in the first place.

A lack of acknowledgement or failing to pay attention to the customer is sending her a message loud and clear: "I don't care about you or your money, and you're not worth my time." If you send this message enough, then it's true that you won't have to be interrupted by a pesky customer, because you'll be *out of business*. And remember that unemployment insurance only lasts twenty-six weeks.

Are you friendly? Customers can easily form an impression as to whether we are "friendly folk" or if we are in the Oscar the Grouch fan club. They form this opinion face to face, and the telltale sign is whether you greet them with a smile. Are you expressionless, or are you frowning?

A smile conveys confidence and helps to build trust. This is true universally. When I'm in a foreign country, even if I can't speak the language, a smile is a way of communicating, and when the person smiles back, I feel like it is a safe environment. One of my clients is located in India, where I travel once a year. Even though I am from a different culture and continent, a smile seems to give a sense of oneness that we are all human beings and have a mutual respect for each other.

I recall a quote by W.C. Fields, one of the greatest comedians of our time. He said, "Start off every day with a smile and get it over with." I think too many people have adopted this philosophy. So many folks seem so unhappy today, spending most of their days frowning or expressionless.

We need to lighten up and smile. Greeting someone with a smile sets a friendly tone from the beginning. Now this may not be good advice if you're a veterinarian and you have to inform little Johnny that his pet hamster just bit the dust. Thankfully, however, most of us are not in those types of situations very often, if ever.

I recently conducted a two-and-a-half-day seminar at the Hyatt Hotel at the Inner Harbor in Baltimore, Maryland, where I encountered some of the best customer service I've ever experienced. Let me share with you some of the things they did exceptionally well.

- Every employee I came in contact with—whether it was the bellman unloading my luggage, the staff member behind the front desk or the maids I passed in the hall every morning—made eye contact, smiled and said "good morning" "hello" or some other appropriate greeting.
- In the seminar room, every person servicing that room introduced himself to me—not just the food and catering manager but also the folks refilling the water pitchers during break. Each one introduced himself and asked if there was anything else he could do for me.
- People kept checking back throughout the day to ensure that everything was on track, and they were always wearing smiles on their faces.

I have been in hundreds of hotels, and I must say that my experience at this particular Hyatt was top notch. I guarantee you that the positive, friendly and helpful attitude that everyone exhibited started at the top in this organization and was a cornerstone of their customer service training program.

Plus, this type of behavior can lead to more business. Since everyone I had come in contact with was so concerned about my satisfaction, there was no reason not to continue the experience. Four associates and I decided to have dinner in their restaurant atop the hotel. Yes, it was one of the best dining experiences I've ever had in a hotel.

I recall conducting a session once in which I made the point that it takes only a few muscles to smile but more than seventy muscles to frown. A fellow in the back of the room raised his hand and said, "So what's wrong with a little exercise?" Ah, the world is just filled with positive people.

When you're smiling, pay attention to the people around you; don't be surprised if your smile becomes contagious. Smiling is like yawning. Once one person starts, others join in. So remember: It's up to you to start the whole world smiling, one person at a time.

Verbal Impressions

Is there enthusiasm in your tone of voice? The vocal tones that come pouring out of our mouths are extremely important to successful communication. Have you ever had the unfortunate experience of having to sit through a presentation by someone who had a monotone voice that could put you fast asleep? Then you ask yourself, "Where was this person when I was tossing and turning for hours last Wednesday night?" Or if you were a fan of the television series *The Wonder Years*, you probably remember the high school science teacher and his monotone voice. His voice could have even kept Rip Van Winkle from ever waking up.

Tone of voice is sometimes equated with the term, "vocal vitality," which refers to how much life comes across in your voice. I'm not saying that you need to be peppy all the time when speaking, but it is important to allow your tone to fluctuate. Sameness is the problem to avoid. Your tone of voice needs to go up and down during a conversation. You need to emphasize some parts of your speech and de-emphasize others.

Another very important point is that you can never raise your voice in anger, no matter how unreasonable a customer may be. Arguing back is like adding gasoline to the fire. The fire will only intensify or rage out of control. One strategy for dealing with an angry customer is to let him vent and get it out of his system. Don't interrupt. Apologize for the problem, and then seek a solution. Keep in mind that when a customer is angry, he probably isn't upset with you but the situation. Don't take his anger personally. Remember that the customer isn't always right but that he is always the customer.

How courteous are you? It is amazing how quickly manners have declined in our society. It's rare these days to hear a "please" or a "thank you," especially among younger children. Given that I travel quite often in my profession, I have the occasion to eat meals out more than most people, and I like to observe how children, teens and young adults act in restaurants.

When the wait staff serves young customers, it's rare that I hear a "thank you" or hear someone say something like, "Could I please have more iced tea?" When the meal is served, it isn't unusual for the customer to not even acknowledge the wait staff.

However, I hesitate to say that young people have poor manners, because at that age, they don't know how to act unless they are taught. Therefore, their lack of responsiveness isn't only their fault but the fault of the adults who need to remind them and lead by example. Therein lies the problem. There usually isn't an example to follow, because the adults have eliminated "please" and "thank you" from their vocabularies, too.

Another important factor relating to courtesy is to always use a person's formal name when addressing him or her. Always say "Mr." or "Ms." Never call someone by his or her first name unless you are given permission.

Let me elaborate. Say you are going to address me. You look at my name tag, and you don't have a clue how to pronounce "Jakielo." Not to fret; anyone with a difficult last name knows he has a hard-to-pronounce name and usually won't leave you hanging. Here is how you would handle that situation. When you go to pronounce my name, just say, "Mr...." Then pause and wait. I'll understand that you are having trouble with my last name, and one of two things will happen. I'll either pronounce my last name for you or say, "Just call me Dave." An alternative would be to try to pronounce my last name as best you can and say, "I hope I pronounced your name correctly."

In the above instance, if I say, "Call me Dave," I am giving you permission to do so. But don't just hand my credit card back to me and say, "Here, Dave" if permission wasn't granted. This may seem like a small thing to you, but in may be an important point to the customer. This is important to remember. Never call a customer by his first name unless he gives you permission. Some customers may interpret your calling them by their first name as a lack of respect.

How helpful are you? This is another important measure of how customers rate service levels.

Let me share with you an experience I had with my daughter Amy at a branch of our local library. It was a Friday, and the teacher had assigned a weekend paper on Shakespeare. So Amy headed off to the library to get a book about the playwright. She headed for the shelf where the book she wanted should have been located. But it wasn't there. After a few minutes of searching to make sure that it wasn't misfiled, she decide to ask the librarian if the book had been checked out.

The librarian checked the computer and discovered that the book was on one of the bookmobiles that was visiting different schools in the city. Amy expressed her disappointment to the librarian, telling her how she had hoped the book was there, because the report was due on Monday. She headed home to consider other options for finding the necessary information. She would lose grade points if she only used information from the Internet, but she figured she was stuck.

About twenty minutes after arriving at home, the phone rang. It was the local librarian, who informed Amy that she had located the bookmobile that had the book and that it was on its way to the library. She told Amy that if she could get to the library before closing time, she would have the book for her. Wow! What an example of customer service!

This librarian, without prompting from anyone, took the initiative and went the extra mile to locate and arrange for Amy to have the book for her report. I think this is amazing, considering that:

- This wasn't a transaction that would lead to a sale or additional profit.
- Amy didn't request that the librarian try to locate the book.
- The action taken wasn't described in any policy or procedure manual. It was just individual initiative.

Unfortunately, this type of service is the exception instead of the rule and is a pleasant contrast to the remarks we hear so often, like, "It's not my department" or "Sorry. Company policy doesn't permit refunds."

How knowledgeable are you? In some businesses, the term "knowledgeable employee" is considered an oxymoron. Today, businesses are faced with higher employee turnover rates than in past decades. One reason is that there are so many choices for employment within the same service setting.

Strolling through your local mall, you can see help wanted signs in every other retailer's window. If an employee doesn't like working for you, she can find another position on her lunch hour. Granted, she may be making a lateral move, but many employees in these retail establishments are just there for the job and paycheck; they aren't working toward a career goal. It doesn't seem to matter to them if they are working for Candles 'R' Us or Clothes 'R' Us.

Given that turnover has increased or has the potential to increase, some employers have abandoned training programs for their employees. Their excuse is, "Why should I spend time and money training an employee? No sooner do I get them trained, they leave." My response is, "Okay, so you don't train them, and they stay. Which approach is more dangerous?"

How many times have you found yourself leaving a store without spending a cent because no one could answer your questions about the product? A lack of employee knowledge can lead to dollars unspent in your establishment, and those dollars will go into your competitors' pockets if they have invested in training.

The popularity of Internet shopping is due in part to the consumer's frustration with not getting help in retail stores. Potential customers figure that if they're buying blind, they might as well do it on the Internet rather than get frustrated trying to deal with inept salespeople.

You may be asking yourself, "How does a customer make the determination that I am knowledgeable?" Keep this very important concept in mind: Employees don't need to know the answer to every question that may be asked of them; however, they need to know where to find the answers.

Companies may not be willing to invest in extensive training programs, but at a minimum, they need to have strong orientation programs so the employees know which departments do what. They must also be instructed what to do when faced with questions they can't answer. They need to know who their "go-to" person is. If there isn't a go-to person available, train them to ask if they can write down the customer's question and have someone get back to her as soon as possible.

This simple step is a better way of handling a customer inquiry than responding, "I don't know." A customer may not be happy with the lack of an answer, but the fact that you offered to try to get an answer should make her less upset or frustrated with an employee's lack of knowledge.

Where Has Customer Service Gone?

Another important area that deals with first impressions is the customer service phone line—or, as I like to refer to it, "automated phone attendant hell." You call a specific phone number provided by the company for customer questions, and you are greeted with a plethora of choices.

Here is a typical recording. "Thank you for calling XYZ Auto Dealership. Please listen to all the choices, because our options have recently changed. Yes, they been increased from the sensible two choices to eight options."

Initial greeting: "If you are calling from a rotary phone, you are a loser. Go find a real phone and call back.

If you are calling about buying a Chevrolet, GMC, Buick or Pontiac, press 1.

If you are calling about buying a Mazda, Toyota, Nissan or horse, press 2.

If you are calling because you want to spend more money on service, press 3.

If you are calling because you want to spend money on bodywork, press 4.

If you are calling to find out about our current bait-and-switch promotions, press 5.

If you are calling because you bought a lemon, please hang up.

If you are calling to speak to a real person, I'm sorry; that is not a valid option.

If you like to waste more time listening to the choices again, press 6."

I find it hard to believe that automated phone attendants actually save companies money. You have the original system cost and the ongoing maintenance on the system plus the lost customers do to frustration or intimidation. Here's a novel idea: Why not have a person answer the phone?

Many businesses are like lemmings; they buy automated systems because the others have bought them. I'm not saying all systems are bad. They are very helpful when it comes to businesses like credit card companies. You can find out you balance, last payment and past transactions any time, night or day. However, when dealing with businesses that normally conduct business face to face, it gives the impression that the company doesn't value you enough to have a real person answer your questions.

It's important to have written policies and procedures. The need for written polices and procedures relating to how we deal with customers is critical in any business. We need to keep in mind that a majority of the workforce is clueless when it comes to techniques and tactics relating to customer satisfaction.

This skill is rarely taught at any level of our educational institutions. When I have asked managers to see their customer service policies and procedures manual, some respond, "We don't have a written manual. Providing customer service is common sense." How can a business rely on common sense? Common sense is defined in the dictionary as "sound and prudent but often-unsophisticated judgment." This definition includes the words "sound" and "prudent," both of which are usually developed through experience. But how can someone entering the workforce, who has not been trained in or exposed to customer service techniques, apply sound and prudent judgment? Without guidance, you're bound to rely on unsophisticated judgment.

This is why it is imperative to have a well-documented manual on how to deal with customers and give detailed examples of how to handle particular situations or problems that may arise. Remember that the managers need to read this manual, too.

It all starts with hiring. In today's marketplace, I realize that it is sometimes difficult to find the right person for the job. The panic to fill an open position has caused some businesses to lower their standards for what they consider the ideal employee. Lowering your standards to fill a position may seem like you have solved a problem, but unfortunately, you probably have created a bigger problem.

The number one quality you should look for in any prospective employee is his or her attitude. Over the years, I have interviewed hundreds of potential candidates, and the one quality I look for in every one is the type of attitude he or she exudes. If a person has the right attitude, I can teach or train him to handle almost any position.

The one thing I have never been able to teach, however, is how to have a positive attitude. A person must make up his or her own mind to have a positive attitude. Abraham Lincoln once said, "A person is about as happy as they make up their mind to be." A key ingredient to hiring a great employee is to hire one that possesses a positive attitude. You can't take a person with a negative attitude and expect him to deliver customer satisfaction. Your attitude always comes through; you can't hide it.

When I meet a job candidate for the first time, I check out his attitude first. If, in the first few minutes of the interview, he comes across as negative or neutral, I know he isn't the type of employee I'm looking for. And it is a challenge to continue the interview and seem interested.

Don't forget about recognition. It's important to keep in mind that employees don't just work for a paycheck; they work for recognition, too. People are motivated by recognition, and they have a need to feel valued. How can you expect an employee to always say "thank you" to a customer and mean it if he never hears a "thank you" from his manager? Just as customers expect recognition, so do our employees.

How would you fill in the blank in the following statement? "My boss never talks to me unless I do something ____." No matter where I am in the world, when I ask people to complete this question, everyone responds in unison with the same answer: "wrong." What a sad commentary this is on today's management style. Many employees equate talking to their boss as a negative experience. We all need to keep in mind what Ken Blanchard stated in his writings. "Every day, make it a point to catch people doing something right and praise them for it."

It's safe to assume that employees will treat customers the same way they are treated by their managers. If internal customer service between managers and employees doesn't exist, it won't exist between employees and customers either.

I would like to conclude by relating a situation that occurred recently in one of the customer satisfaction seminars I was conducting in California. Right before our morning break, I was asking the question, "Why it is so hard to find good customer service?" and then I explained that we need to have written guidelines for employees to follow. At the break, a fellow approached and said, "I know why good customer service is hard to find." I asked him why, and he made what I consider a valid point: "Think about it. People entering the work force today have probably never experienced good customer service." Today, young workers have only experienced self-service or lack of service. They weren't customers back in the day when salespeople were knowledgeable about their products and services. They don't know differently, so when they take on a position in today's work-force, they are as unresponsive as the people to whom they have been exposed.

It's sad but true. Today, the majority of the public says the most important part of any transaction is the *price*, and we always want the lowest one possible. This doesn't come without a sacrifice, and that sacrifice is that businesses aren't going to increase their cost by investing money in training.

Therefore, we need to keep in mind that we are only going to get the level of customer service we are willing to pay for, and if we want rock-bottom prices that are offered by the mega stores of today, we must accept rock-bottom service.

David Jakielo

Dave Jakielo, has been speaking, consulting and teaching successful business methods to managers, clerical staffs, business owners and other professionals throughout the country and in England and India. Dave has extensive experience in sales, marketing, business start-ups and turnarounds, acquisitions assimilation, customer service and negotiations. He is co-author of the books; The Sales Coach.. Tips from the Pros and the book Information Technology for the Practicing Physician. He is also a monthly columnist in the trade journal Billing. Dave received his CHBME (Certified Healthcare Billing & Management Executive) in 1998. Dave's professional membership includes, Past President of the Healthcare Billing & Management Association (HBMA). Past President of the National Speakers Association Pittsburgh Chapter, plus a member of the International Brotherhood of Magicians. Dave is a graduate of University of Pittsburgh and received his Masters in Management from Carnegie Mellon University. Plus he is a certified trainer. He has trained at the Buckley School of Public Speaking. He is President of his own Seminar, Training and Consulting Company.

David Jakielo
Seminars & Consulting
86 Hall Avenue
Pittsburgh PA 15205
412-921-0976
Email: Dave@DavidJakielo.com

Chapter Nine

The Cost of Consumer Silence

Celeste M. Warner, MA, CPCC

Introduction: Complaining Can Be Kind

In conversations I've had with thousands of Americans across the country about customer service, there is a simple yet powerful theme that runs through each dialogue. Customer service in America stinks. The most content of American consumers can count on their right hands the number of businesses that constantly wow them with exemplary customer service. The rest of us consumers are beaten down by the daily habits of service people ignoring us, doing the bare minimum and wasting valuable hours of our time. So many people are tempted to scream, just like in the movie *Network*, "I'm mad as hell, and I'm not going to take it any more!"

But we don't scream. On average, we don't even complain—not even a little. In fact, some of us lie. When we receive poor service and are asked how everything is, we routinely say "good" or "fine." This silence of ours costs our country hundreds of thousands of jobs and hundreds of thousands of dollars in trade. It could position America as a less attractive partner in the international marketplace. This silence is not deafening, but it appears to be falling on deaf ears, and the silence we keep masks the only power we consumers have over the deaf masses of service providers.

Like everyone else, I, too, am angry about poor service. But I am equally angry when my friends are unemployed because American businesses have to downsize or move to another country. I am even angrier with managers who allow this to happen. I get angry at my fellow Americans over their low expectations for service and for not speaking up and not protecting American businesses from themselves. I want them to break the silence and speak the truth—even complain—before it's too late.

We could encourage our friends and families to complain. We could tell businesses exactly what we want from them. We could explain to them how we want to be treated by their employees at all levels. We could tell them that if they don't change, we will no longer support them. We could rally around great businesses. We as consumers could put local businesses on probation until they shape up. We could take responsibility for helping American businesses stay in business. However, the shocking truth is that we *are* American businesses. We are the people providing poor service. We are the people who are ignoring and losing customers.

Statistically, a few outspoken individuals complain constantly. Others complain only when they've "had enough." My challenge is unique. I want to help consumers complain to the customer service representative the *first* time service is less than exemplary. My goal for us consumers is to view complaining as the kindest, most loving thing we could do for our country and the businesses that support it. If giving and receiving feedback in its kindest forms became a way of life for Americans, what would the possibilities be for our personal lives? I'm asking you to join me in making this happen for our country, your business and for yourself. If we don't, we will miss some amazing personal and professional opportunities.

If successful in my campaign against consumer silence, I will have helped businesses like yours find unique ways to motivate their individual types of customers. I would encourage consumers to take charge of the success of businesses in their own communities as well as throughout the country. The message I send to consumers is: "Show Your Love for American Businesses—Tell Them How They Can Serve You Better."

Background for This Chapter: Years of Research

A number of national and international experts have impacted my thinking and training programs over the years. For a complete list, please refer to the references I have listed at the end of this chapter. What follows is a combination of formal and field-based research that has guided me to create the program of service excellence I am now presenting to you.

Although the definition of "excellent service" is hard to wrap your mind around, it's easy to recognize when it is missing. About twelve years ago, long before this book came to be, I became interested in helping companies deliver excellent customer service. For example, I designed a customer service training program based on the following assumption: If we simply treat our own customers the way we want to be treated, then poor customer service would be a thing of the past. This program was called TLC—Think Like the Customer.

To help company teams in my audiences to think like the customer, I asked them to think about their own sets of customer service pet peeves. The following three complaints were reported by each audience with which I worked: People hate waiting, being ignored (another time waster) and customer representatives who are rude or who become defensive about customer feedback.

After fifty or more presentations to healthcare managers and front-line staff from across the country, these responses were used to help teams create internal policies to counteract what we as consumers hate most. To counteract being ignored and having time wasted, these teams created greeting policies that described in detail the manner and the time limit in which to greet customers. To counteract rudeness and defensive behavior, they also created problem-solving policies. These policies described in detail the words, body language and tone to be used when met with negative feedback, an expressed concern or simple feedback. Immediately handling negative feedback in a positive, appreciative manner helps build personal relationships with customers. A properly handled problem produces trust. In fact, statistics suggest (Blanchard 1999) that customers are actually more loyal after they have had a problem taken care of than if they'd never had a problem at all.

Businesses should view themselves as vessels for customer feedback and concerns. Their customers should say to themselves and others, "I always do business with _____. No matter what the problem is, they always fix it." The actual wording of the policies is relatively unimportant. It is the existence of the policies themselves, the spirit in which they are delivered and the problems that are prevented by using them that is important. People don't simply respond to what you are doing or saying; they respond to who you are being as a person. Customers can tell whether or not you are following a formula or being sincere in your desire to fix their problem. These personalized policies were created by the individual team members who would be carrying out the policies.

These teams had created a simple customer feedback cause-and-effect loop, beginning with a customer providing feedback. The customer is met by a customer service representative who responds positively to the feedback. This positive response turns the unhappy customer into a happy one who is willing to risk giving feedback again if necessary because of this positive experience. The early TLC Program removed from a customer/service representative interaction what we disliked and inserted what we did like. However, this early program proved incomplete. It turned out to be only half of the equation.

This is my first recommendation to you. Create your own Think Like the Customer (TLC) program at your business. Ask your teams to design a standard and consistent way to greet people and respond to problems, complaints or concerns. Put this design in the form of a policy, and make it part of all orientations, job descriptions and evaluations. Remember that this is only the first step.

The second half of the equation is getting a consumer who is highly motivated to provide feedback to businesses. The question becomes, "How can consumers be motivated to do this? How could we motivate people to trust us more and take the precious time they have to help us improve our businesses?"

Ultimately, the above thinking and questions are what led me to pursue this issue.

Customer Silence is Poison

According to John Goodman of Technical Research Programs, Inc.—as reported in William Davidow and Bro Uttal's (1990) *Total Customer Service*, a study of the complaint process at more than 300 companies and government agencies—somewhere between two and four percent of all dissatisfied customers complain. Goodman claims that feedback of any kind only comes from the most satisfied and most dissatisfied customers. Janelle Barlow and Claus Moller (1996) found that only one in twenty-seven people complains about poor service to the service provider. Paradoxically, on average, the remaining twenty-six each tells sixty-seven other people about a poor service experience, and we as providers never really know what is going on. Customer service guru Paul Timm (1989) arrived at the number sixty-seven by studying our behavior. He says an average dissatisfied consumer tells about eleven other people who, in turn, tell five or six others each and so on. This totals sixty-seven people who hear about one negative customer service experience. A.C. Nielsen Co. surveyed customers of a food processor to find out if they complained when they were dissatisfied. They found that only two percent of unhappy customers complained. Thirty-four percent quietly switched brands. (Davidow 1990) Nielsen's figures provide us with very disconcerting information. Given that 40,000 customers had complained to the manufacturer, it is likely that two million customers were dissatisfied and that 760,000 switched brands. According to Nielsen, sixty-eight percent of customers switch because of the indifference of the salesperson. Only fourteen percent of customers switch over dissatisfaction with the product. (Davidow 1990)

Effective Systems For Service Delivery Improve Service

Ken Blanchard (1999), author of *Customer Service Insider Secrets*, says satisfied customers just aren't good enough. Satisfied customers walk. Businesses should find a way to create "raving fans." Raving fans aren't simply satisfied customers. Raving fans are customers who are so thrilled with your service that they actually sell for you. The goal of a customer-service-focused company should be to turn all of its customers into unpaid salespeople, according to Blanchard. To do this, he emphasizes that businesses must create and implement "nifty systems."

Nifty systems begin to take shape when a business decides what it really wants to look like and feel like to its customers. Once this decision is made, the business needs to create a "vision of perfection" centered on the customer. Once that vision becomes real, businesses need to find out what their customers really want and alter their vision if necessary. The last rule Blanchard stresses for creating nifty systems is to deliver the vision plus one percent. Adding one percent keeps the systems flexible and alive. These systems need to be consistent throughout the business. They need to be simple and only enhanced when they become habits for each and every employee. This is a huge challenge for business people. How can you motivate employees so that they want to grow and better themselves personally and professionally? Blanchard warns that "wowing" (Peters 1994) customers one day, only to disappoint them the next, is worse then never wowing them at all. Tom Peters also adds that wowing customers should be the specific focus of any business interested in keeping and acquiring customers.

Peter Senge (1995), from the MIT Learning Organization talks about Blanchard's nifty systems and describes the process of creating these as "systems thinking." Imagine that a business knows that it has a service problem in one area. Systems thinking moves from looking at who in the organization is doing something wrong to what is wrong or missing in the organization's business processes and systems as well as what the business can do to fix the problem. Systems thinking allows us to remove blame in our organizations. If it's a systems problem, employees won't feel embarrassed when asked to report complaints or concerns, because they know that they will no longer be blamed for what went wrong. Senge also says that systems problems are circular. They go around and around and continue until the problem is fixed. He adds that every circle tells a story; you can pick any business problem and know that it is part of an ongoing circle of events. Systems thinking helps us understand that complex feedback processes are circular and can generate problematic patterns of behavior within organizations.

This feedback process is similar to what takes place with the thermostat in your home. If it gets cold, your thermostat turns on and warms you. When it warms to the settings you've chosen, the heat shuts off. This feedback is ongoing and circular. The problem with this example is that the customer service professional cannot always tell when the customer is getting "cold" and often doesn't have the chance to "warm" up the environment for the customer. Customers normally wait until the third or fourth time to complain—that is, if they complain at all. This makes it very hard to see what really caused the customer to be dissatisfied.

Accordingly, these circular systems (or "loops," as they will be referred to throughout the rest of this chapter) can be either reinforcing or balancing. A reinforcing loop that could interfere with a business's ability to provide great service might look like the following:

1) A customer complains. 2) An unskilled person handles the complaint poorly and doesn't inform those who could prevent that

same problem from occurring in the future. 3) The disenchanted customer tells everyone he/she knows about the poor service. 4) The business loses customers. 5) Another customer complains. 6) The cycle continues again and again. 7) The company goes out of business. Reinforcing loops tend to accelerate creating a downward spiral for the business.

A balancing loop—which includes fixing the initial problem but not fixing the root cause that might interfere with a business's ability to provide great service—might look like the following:

1) A customer complains. 2) A trained customer service professional creates a solution that satisfies the customer. 3) There is no system for forwarding complaints, or there are poorly trained managers who don't know how to use the information. 4) A different customer complains about the same issue. 5) A trained customer service professional creates a solution that satisfies the customer. 6) The cycle continues. 7) The business never really makes money. 8) A competitor with better systems drives them out of business. (Senge 1995)

These two types of loops are both examples of unproductive ways in which many businesses work. Business people need to understand the various loops in their organizations to help see how everything counts. As business professionals, we need to understand the impact of our every behavior. Everything counts, from the smiles on our faces to the shine on our shoes to the feelings in our hearts. It is that to which customers respond. Senge (1995) says that our lack of awareness concerning our impact is often caused by the fact that cause and effect are often separated by time and space. We need to raise our level of awareness about our behaviors and see the impact occurring days, months or even years later. He advocates that businesses engage in systems thinking in order to create the kind of experiences they want for their customers. To be systems thinkers, business professionals must raise the level of awareness concerning their own personal impact. They must also understand that every circle tells a story and see the reinforcing and balancing loops clearly in their business.

Excellent Customer Service is a Two-Way Street

Motivating people to complain or give feedback as a strategic tool for businesses has been studied and taught by Barlow and Moller (1996), who co-authored *A Complaint is a Gift*. In it, they highlight many ways to motivate customers to voice feedback. They include many of the traditional methods like toll-free numbers, comment cards and suggestion boxes. They suggest that most business people view customer feedback as negative and therefore respond to the feedback in a defensive manner. They conclude that if business people view a complaint as a gift or something positive, they might not be defensive when feedback is given. Showing appreciation to customers for feedback would positively affect the customer's experience.

My second recommendation to you is to start thinking about what might motivate your unique set of customers to want to give you feedback and improve the current service you provide. What also might motivate your staff to bring complaints and concerns forward so that they don't happen again? Examine the rewards you give to employees who bring negative information to you. Do you reward truth or employee silence? Remember once again that we are still in the early stages of creating a system that will work.

Engineering customers' experiences are what the future of customer service is all about, according to Lewis Carbone (1984), president of Experience Engineering Co. Customers always get an experience along with a product or service. Sadly, many of the experiences we have as consumers are negative. This is because businesses don't understand that they are in the customer service business. Many businesses believe they only sell a product or service. They forget about the experience customers receive while interacting with them during the purchase of products or services. Companies need to incorporate the customer experience into the business design. This means taking feedback from customers and recreating the experience for them from start to finish by design. Businesses and business people alike need to ask the question, "What is the experience of being with me and doing business with me really like?"

Business guru Michael J. Wolf (1999), in *The Entertainment Economy*, suggests that once service providers understand what consumers really want, they will soon understand that the sky is the limit and that great service can be very profitable. Consumers are all doing more things with less time. Nearly half of us would be willing to spend more money to save time. Also because we are all working so hard, we are willing to pay more money to make purchasing the things we need a fun experience, which Wolf refers to as "hedonomics." He says that if business people can make the purchase of products or services fun and entertaining, they will have created loyal customers.

In order to best understand and utilize the ideas provided by the above experts, I needed to incorporate their thinking into my own.

The Initial TLC Program Became the Predecessor of "Show Your Love"

The early TLC program was implemented and evaluated in a Vermont-based nursing home. I am describing this evaluation process, because I believe the customer service policies we implemented are very similar to the current policies you have in your businesses. These policies are very important to have, but unless they are supported by lots of consumer feedback, which is self-supported, they will not be as successful as you need them to be.

This Vermont program was evaluated in the fall of 1999. The evaluation indicated that internal customer service systems, which included greeting and problem solving policies, were not sufficient to sustain long-term change. These greeting and problem-solving policies were designed to counter what consumers hate most. There seemed to be a breakdown between the service provided by business people and the service expected by consumers. These results led to redesigning the system. The results of this evaluation pointed to what was missing from the initial feedback loop.

The simple feedback loop between the customer and the service representative in the early TLC program did not include the many other steps and questions that now seem vital. The missing steps included a system for gathering feedback, quantifying and qualifying feedback, making positive changes for the customer based on this feedback and informing customers of these changes. This early, incomplete loop began with customer feedback. A trained customer service representative responded properly to the feedback, and the customer went away happy. The simple loop, although in place, wasn't working. In some cases, the early loop was a small balancing loop. It began with customer feedback that was met with a grateful customer service professional. This balancing loop helped the customer feel good about giving feedback but did not ensure that the original issue that caused the feedback would not occur again. In other cases, the early loop was a reinforcing loop. It began with a customer providing feedback. This customer was not thanked or appreciated. The issue that caused the feedback continued, and the dissatisfied customer told many others about the poor service.

The early, simple loop did not encourage sufficient customer feedback in the long run. It continued to support consumer silence. This silence gives many businesses false hope about the real problems in their organizations. If Moller (1996) is correct, twenty-six out of twenty-seven customers do not provide feedback to businesses but go elsewhere to do their business. Businesses need to understand the implications of these statistics.

Some of the effects of customer silence can be seen by considering the following:

- Add the lost dollars associated with the "lifetime value" of each of the twenty-six silent customers. Then add the cost of bringing on the new customers needed to replace the lost customers.
- Then add the lost dollars associated with the twenty-six silent customers telling an average of sixty-seven others about their negative experiences.
- Then add the lifetime value the business would have had in profits if it hadn't lost the original customer and the lifetime value of the sixty-seven others.
- Then add the lost future profits from lost future purchases and lost future referrals associated with these lost customers.
- Lastly, multiply the final sum by the number of negative complaints the business receives.

Businesses that took the time to do the simple calculations above would soon see the size of the problem and understand why a system that welcomes and rewards feedback is a necessary investment.

> My third recommendation is to create a system for gathering feedback (if given), quantifying and qualifying feedback, making positive changes for the customer based on this feedback and informing customers of these changes. Sadly, unless customers are willing to give feedback, we will still lose countless dollars due to their silence.

The early TLC program, much like many of the current customer service policies you may have in place, missed the mark in many ways, because it didn't factor in the intricacies of consumer behavior. I needed to learn more, so I conducted two sets of interviews with some highly successful business professionals. I found some interesting information about how we as business people think.

Initial interviews showed a disconnect between the role of consumer and the role of business person.

An important question needed answering if the program was to be successfully designed: If business people in the role of consumer can consistently name what they dislike about poor service, then why aren't they great service providers? Most consumers want better customer service from business people. Successful business people were interviewed and asked about this problem. The interview structure required a two-step thinking process. First, each interviewee was asked to think as a businessperson and project how customers might answer these questions; second, each was asked to answer the questions once more, this time wearing his own consumer hat. In order to do this kind of thinking, business people would need to be honest with themselves and see the questions from two distinct perspectives. The results of these questions showed that business people did not make the leap to understanding how contrary these two perspectives could be.

They were asked the following questions: Why should customers give feedback? What would be the benefits to your business if customers gave feedback when they were dissatisfied? What could make them give more feedback? Why don't they give feedback? What might stop someone from giving feedback to you? What's the best way to provide feedback? What could happen if customers don't give feedback?

I then asked them to think about their own consumer behaviors. Why should you give feedback? What would be the benefits of giving feedback?

While in the role of consumer, they could easily respond to what bothers them about poor service. Their responses were very similar to the large number of public responses received across the country. They noted that time wasting and defensive behaviors were disturbing. Yet when asked how they behaved as consumers, they said that they, too, remained silent, even when they were dissatisfied. They, like most consumers, didn't give feedback, because they didn't believe it worked. These beliefs are prevalent throughout our culture. People need to see that the changes they have suggested have been put into practice. Without this evidence, they are left believing that providing feedback is not a good use of their time.

These individuals represented a cross-section of American businesses, from "Mom and Pop" shops to one of the largest Internet service providers in the country. One individual was involved in several successful fast-food enterprises and is currently a vice president with a national chain. In his interview, he remarked that, "Pleasing the customer is the whole point of my business." Another individual was the manager of a retail shop, following a career in the research and development industry, from which he retired as VP of business development. He said he enjoyed interacting with customers on a personal basis and believed a business should work hard to please its customers. One twenty-year veteran of the retail business confided that she prizes the personal relationship she has with her customers, and she believes that customers give more feedback than they used to but do so in an ineffective way that has left her unsure of the real problem. Her customers say things like, "I'm not finding the types of products I want here anymore." This type of feedback is vague, and this owner needs to develop communication skills to get to the real issues.

The interviewees said they were committed to pleasing their customers and to providing the best possible experience for them that they could. Yet they showed a real lack of proactive solicitation of customer interaction that would greatly enhance customer satisfaction and, therefore, bottom-line business performance. In addition, all of them, when imagining themselves as customers instead of business people, showed a remarkable passivity about their own satisfaction as customers. While most of them saw the importance of giving feedback, they were willing to walk away dissatisfied after a single try. This behavior suggested a lack of connection between their role as consumer and their role as business person. One conclusion that could be drawn from these interviews is that even very successful people need a better understanding of the effects of consumer silence.

The Second Interviews Show a Misunderstanding of the Problem

I interviewed forty-six teams of business people in October 2000, asking them the following question: "If we as consumers dislike how business people treat us, then why don't we as business people treat consumers better? In essence, why don't we TLC—Think Like the Customer?" The first group of interviewees mentioned above saw no connection between their behaviors and their customers'.

The second set of interviewees, described below, offered different perspectives about customer service when presented with the problem. The large numbers of similar responses from these interviews were striking. There are important reasons that business people can't TLC. Thirty-seven out of forty-six teams believed that upper managers were poorly trained and that they didn't support front-line managerial and policy changes. In essence, this means that even though a customer service policy is implemented, managers do not lead by example or actually discipline and manage around these programs. This lack of leadership may derive from the fact that managers don't fully understand the importance of successful customer service systems and the importance of consumer feedback. My hunch is that this may be one reason that the initial TLC program was sometimes less successful than desired. In addition to there being an outcry for trained managers, there were opinions by these managers that suggested revisiting the systems thinking in the initial TLC program. Twenty of the forty-six teams claimed that top management, in addition to being untrained, actually treated staff poorly. For example, how were staff supposed to be motivated to treat customers well when they were treated so poorly themselves?

Twenty-five out of the forty-six teams said that there were no systems for gathering, quantifying and responding to feedback. These were serious places where internal systems broke down. With no system, and worse, no authority to really handle customer feedback, their hands were tied. Twenty-six of the forty-six teams believed that customers were interested only in price. This thinking runs counter to the research presented by Wolf (1999), who found that customers would actually be willing to pay more money for better service.

The teams also said that their top managers believed that customers weren't giving feedback, because everything was fine with their service. At the same time, twenty-eight of the forty-six teams said that customers didn't know how to give feedback correctly. If consumers did give feedback effectively, according to these teams, then service representatives would be more willing to pay attention and fix the problems. Against all of the research on consumer silence I had shared with them, members of these teams thought that the amount of feedback that they currently received was accurate. These responses helped point to the problems with the initial system. Some of the early problems came from the erroneous assumptions evident in the initial design.

Erroneous Assumptions Concerning Consumers Need to be Corrected

Assumptions about consumer behavior can greatly affect the way we view and solicit feedback. Barlow and Moller's (1996) advice to use suggestion boxes and comment cards for soliciting feedback misses many of the problems associated with consumer silence. These methods are prevalent in most businesses today. Consumers see comment cards in restaurants and hotels and often get letters telling their customers, "Let us know how you feel." Even with these vehicles welcoming feedback, consumers remain silent. In my opinion, these methods are outdated and are not going to produce the kind of information businesses need to stay in business. My research shows that people will not use these vehicles to provide feedback unless they are highly motivated to do so.

Poor service and the poor handling of feedback alone are not the only barriers to consumers who might be willing to provide feedback. Other equally powerful reasons have to do with people not wanting to be perceived as complainers and with people viewing giving positive feedback as a waste of time. The grand scale impact that would be needed to change consumers' behavior and motivate them to provide feedback would require a different way of thinking about the problem. Experience has taught me that there are other ways that business people create barriers to feedback and communicate to customers that feedback isn't welcome. They say things like, "That's our policy." Many times, the customer is blamed because she didn't send in the warranty card. Customers providing feedback are refused return phone calls, are treated badly when they give feedback and are often passed on to someone else. Other company systems also discourage feedback. Most often, there are no obvious vehicles for feedback, so providing feedback is a struggle for consumers. And even when this is not the case, there is no follow-up. (Barlow 1996) Giving feedback often seems to be what consumers hate most—a waste of time.

Erroneous Assumptions in the Original "Think Like the Customer" System Can Help You

According to Senge's (1995) theory concerning the importance of identifying loops in business, it was easy to see where there were problems in the system. The initial simple and inadequate loop had assumed a customer providing feedback and a trained customer service professional responding positively to the feedback. It now seems apparent that there were two major reasons why the program didn't work well in the long term. 1) The customer had no motivation to give feedback. 2) The trained service professional had no one who was truly interested in learning from the feedback. Based on the second series of interviews, this could be due to a number of reasons, including either no existing systems or the presence of poorly trained managers. The delay in time between the complaint and the lost business blurred the cause and effect, too, even for well-trained managers. There needed to be a way to motivate consumers to give feedback and ensure that this feedback would be appreciated and used.

I believe that this motivation comes from a simple public relations campaign. I have created successful campaigns with many of my clients by having them communicate to their customers the importance of customer help and support concerning their businesses. Their customers are now more than willing to "Show Their Love" via feedback. The captured costs associated with successes have outweighed the costs of implementing this program ten to one.

My fourth recommendation is for you to think about your best and most loyal customers. Reward them for information about their relationship with you. Get humble. Reward customers who tell you about the experiences they've had with you. Ask yourself, "What am I willing to announce to the public about my need for their feedback? Am I willing to ask for help? How grateful am I willing to be for feedback? How can I implement a public relations campaign that would make each of my customers 'Show Their Love' for my business?"

Breaks in the System: Understanding Problems With Most Customer Service Systems and the Early TLC System

Four breaks in the initial system existed.

- The first break was in the simple collection of feedback. Service providers were attempting to fix the service-related problem but were not collecting the feedback. From this first break, the following questions arose. What should the service representative do with the feedback? Who should he tell? Where could he input the data? Whether he used paper or one of the many software-based Customer Relationship Management (CRM) systems, there needed to be a way to gather and use the important information that was now being shared by the company's customers.

- The second break in the system happened when the little bit of data that were actually collected and analyzed still did not produce a change in behavior. These data were often accidentally collected, because the front-line service provider could not solve the problem to the customer's satisfaction, and the customer complained to the business manager or owner. Without this accident, top management would probably not have been aware of the front-line service problems. A customer service policy that would prevent negative feedback from happening again needed to be created. This policy could involve simply looking at each piece of data and looking for ways to improve service based on the data. Companies need to create policies and use the information they receive from customers to make required changes in service, or else customers will continue to believe that giving feedback is a waste of their time.

- The third break in the system happened in two scenarios. First, it happened when service representatives didn't follow the newly-installed policies designed to prevent future negative feedback and when managers didn't hold service representatives accountable for these new behaviors. Well-trained managers were the remedy for this break.
- The fourth break in the system came when the service representatives actually made the changes but never let the customer know about them. This reinforced the idea of demonstrating that their feedback and time were well used.

Once this system is fixed, you are then ready to create your own "Show Your Love" public relations campaign.

The Missing Link—A Public Cry for Help

What was missing from my program (and probably yours) was an educated and motivated consumer who could imagine the possibilities of a superior customer-focused future and could understand the hardship that could come if consumers continue their silence. This consumer would not only know how to give feedback but would also give feedback to businesses that would appreciate receiving it, use the complaint to ensure better service and learn from the business how this feedback was being utilized. Consumers might even be rewarded in some way for the time they took in offering feedback.

I am reminded of a scene from the movie/play *Camelot*. The scene shows the king struggling with trying to create a better way of life in Camelot. He wants to create a new breed of might-filled knights. He wants these knights to perform heroic deeds without misusing their power and accordingly suggests that the old way of thinking of "might as right" needs to be changed to "might for right." That's my hope for consumers. I want them to move from thinking that "complaining is right" to "complaining for right." Consumers should leave behind the old way of thinking that giving feedback means nothing or is negative and move toward believing that "giving feedback means something." If we educate consumers to believe that feedback is kind and loving, giving feedback will be put into a whole new context. Consumers need to believe that they are actually doing something positive for the business, themselves and society as a whole. The degree to which this program can be successful rests on consumers who believe this, are motivated to give feedback and are rewarded once they give it.

One survey asked consumers what it would take to get them to provide more feedback. Although many responded that a discount or gift would be nice, all agreed that they needed proof, a sign that complaining and providing feedback was a good use of their time. Public relations specialist April Williams, the owner of Northstar Marketing in Wickford, Rhode Island, initially suggested a "Help Wanted" sign to signal to consumers that the business displaying the sign would appreciate and reward feedback. The sign read, "Help Wanted: Looking for Consumers to Help American Businesses Deliver Exemplary Customer Service." We then thought that the "Help Wanted" sign might be confusing to people who were looking for work. After many debates and a gathering of opinions, we settled on a sign saying, "Your Right, Your Duty, Your Privilege—Tell the Truth To American Businesses." Consumers who saw the sign in the business's door or window could rest assured that their feedback would be heard and acted on. If successful, the sign would be the next generation Good Housekeeping Seal of Approval. This decision was made before 9/11/01. After 9/11, everything changed, including my approach to motivating consumers. Instead of "Norma Raeing" businesses, I thought it was more important to be on their side. That is when I can up with the "Show Your Love" idea. It is actually motivating consumers to be kinder instead of sharing their anger. It was, indeed, a change for the better.

The "Show Your Love" sign has been displayed in businesses that have implemented the full loop described in this chapter. It begins with customer feedback and ends with feedback to the customer about the changes that have been made, or not made, based on the initial investment of their time.

The new and more complete TLC program I am now recommending includes a customer service training program and a public relations program motivating consumer feedback.

Assessing Your Ability to Implement a Successful TLC Program

By answering an important series of questions, a business is able to assess whether or not the TLC system is a necessary addition to the current interaction with its customers. The answers also point to the amount of commitment a business needs to have in order to successfully maintain the flow of feedback from its customers.

Questions for Businesses Interested in Implementing the TLC Program

What are the current systems your business uses to collect customer feedback? Describe in detail these systems, including how the feedback is handled, how it is measured, how it is used to alter the current system and how the changes are communicated to the customer providing the feedback. What we are attempting is systems thinking. According to Senge (1995), systems thinking helps businesses design systems to create the exact experience they want for their customers. Every loop or circle tells a story about how the business works and the experience the customer has based on the loop we create for him or her.

1. Is this system a balancing loop, like the one described earlier in this chapter?

2. Is this system a reinforcing loop as described earlier?

3. The goal of the TLC Program is to create a reinforcing loop that both accelerates positively and also motivates customer feedback, which, in turn, is positively reinforced. A reinforcing loop that would assist a business's ability to provide great service might look like the following: A) A customer complains. B) A trained customer service representative positively responds to the complaint by showing sincere appreciation and rewarding the feedback. C) The very happy customer tells everyone he/she knows about the excellent service. D) The business gains customers. E) Another customer complains. F) The cycle continues again and again.

4. Are there any hidden messages given to customers that feedback is not welcomed?

5. What system could this business create in order to have a reinforcing loop that positively spirals upward and encourages more and more feedback?

6. In what areas does this business want feedback? What can this business's customers expect from it? What are the standards of service and quality that these customers can count on?

7. What would motivate/reward this business's customers to provide feedback? How should these customers provide feedback? What should they expect when they do?

8. How could this business motivation/reward system be attached and included as part of the newly created upward spiraling reinforcing loop?

The National Public Relations Campaign

I am creating a national public relations campaign designed to support those businesses interested in soliciting more feedback. The objective of the national campaign is simple: Consumers will want to complain to a business showcasing the "Show Your Love for American Businesses—Tell Us How We Can Serve You Better" sign. The negative beliefs, barriers and stereotypes associated with complaining will be addressed during the "Show Your Love" campaign. The complete details of the national campaign are still under consideration. The campaign's focus is to link complaining and feedback to something positive rather than something negative.

The national campaign includes news advisories, news releases, television and radio talk shows, car flyers and door hangers. It also includes a toll-free number and a Web site where customers can complain about customer service horror stories and praise great customer service practices. The news stories will be both motivational and educational. They will focus on the why, how and where to complain.

The Individual Business Campaign

Your own local campaign should mirror the national campaign. Businesses that have put the positive reinforcing loop into action should host their own version of a "Show Your Love" sign everywhere. They should be using the sign as part of their current advertising and letterhead and include it in any correspondence with current and potential customers. They should be sporting the sign on their employees' car windows and handing customers "Show Your Love"-laden business cards with "How to Complain" tips. News releases describing your new philosophy, policies and reward systems should be sent to all your local and regional radio and television stations and newspapers. Individual letters should be sent to current, former and potential clients describing the above and literally pleading for their help and feedback. The reward should be something you know they really want.

Why Should *You* Consider This Program?

I asked myself about all the positives associated with this project. For me, the biggest positive is impacting the way people perceive feedback. If people view feedback and complaints as good, Americans will stay employed, businesses will continue to make money and contribute to our tax base, and we'll all receive better service. Additional positives include service professionals who will no longer be defensive when hearing feedback. The implications for success in their personal lives, thanks to learning this one skill of not taking things personally, could be very powerful.

I also asked myself about the negatives associated with this project. At first glance, other than the hard work and the financial costs of getting the project off the ground, there seemed to be very few negatives. Although I was left with questions, I didn't want to make any assumptions about the potential of people challenged by change. Some of the questions include: Do businesses really care about great service? Would Americans take the time to give feedback to help American businesses? Would this program be viewed as too "Pollyanna-ish" to be taken seriously?

Conclusion

I know that this project is doable. It may not be doable in this original form, but it will be continuously refined and will truly become part of my life's work. I know that my mind will find a way to get the idea across to consumers and business people alike that giving feedback to businesses is good and necessary. I also know that I will find a way to convince businesses to take part in this program. Businesses will hang the "Show Your Love" sign in one form or another. They will save money from the increased knowledge that their customers share with them. I want you to be one of those businesses. Please commit today to look for small ways to include some of this work. Please also give feedback to businesses, even when they don't ask for it or seem to appreciate it. Please give feedback in a way that shows your love for American businesses. I am begging you to invest in yourselves as human beings so that you can be viewed as icons of service and as amazing human beings committed to making our world a better place.

We're all familiar with the expression, "If you are not part of the solution, you are part of the problem." This expression is 100 percent true as it relates to customer service and consumer silence. You are obviously part of the solution if you are still reading this chapter. Good luck.

References

Barlow, Janelle and Claus Moller. A Complaint is a Gift. San Francisco, CA: Berrett- Koehler Publishers, Inc. 1996

Blanchard, Ken et al. Celebrate Customer Service Insider Secrets. Corte Madera, CA: Select Press. 1999.

Carbone, Lewis P. and Stephen H Haeckel. "Shaping the Profession of Marketing" Marketing Management Winter 1994.

Combs, E. and Dan Nimmo. Subliminal Politics: Myths and Mythmakers in America, Englewood, NJ: Prentice Hall. 1980

Davidow, William and Bro Uttal. Total Customer Service. New York, NY: Harper Perennial. 1990.

Levine, Michael. Guerrilla P.R.: How You Can Wage an Effective Publicity Campaign... Without Going Broke. New York, NY: Harper-Collins. 1993.

Peppers, Don and Martha Rogers. Enterprise One to One. New York, NY: DOUBLEDAY. 1997.

Peter, Tom. The Tom Peters Seminar. New York, NY: Vintage Books. 1994.

Senge, Peter, et al. Learning Organizations. Portland, Oregon: Productivity Press. 1995.

Steinberg, Charles S. The Creation of Consent: Public Relations in Practice. New York, NY: Hastings House, 1973

Timm, Paul. The Power of Customer Service. Chicago, IL: Jack Wilson & Associates. 1989.

Wolf, Michael J. The Entertainment Economy. New York, NY: Time Books. 1999.

Celeste M. Warner, MA, CPCC

Celeste M. Warner has personally trained thousands of our nations top executives and middle managers to become high achieving individuals committed to improving their corporate culture and corporate profits. Celeste does this by helping clients identify their areas of personal excellence and "Take Charge" of their lives. One constant separates Celeste's programming from any other experience of its kind. Celeste's unique presentation and delivery style makes people want to listen and learn. She enthusiastically blends humor with time-tested success strategies that help people enjoy their work like never before. Celeste is a professional executive coach from the nationally acclaimed Coaches training Institute in San Rafael, California. She serves as an on-camera trainer and writer for industrial training films and network commercials. Celeste has voiced commercials for USA, CNN, USA and many cable and radio stations. She has directed the marketing and customer service efforts of our Nation's leading healthcare corporations and colleges. She is a member of the National Speakers Association.

Celeste M. Warner, MA, CPCC
President, CMW Training International
169 Cedar Street
Warwick, RI 02818
401.886.8884 office
401.886.1188 fax
Email: celeste@celestemwarner.com
Email: celeste@takechargeofyourlife.net

175

Chapter Ten

Customer Service Go For BROKE!
A Formula For Superior
Call Center Performance

James R. Dawson and
Jennifer M. Dawson

In 1876 Alexander Graham Bell invented the telephone, providing a way to quickly communicate with another person without needing to be physically present. Today, according to CBSNews.com, there are twenty-four billion telemarketing calls made each year nationally, resulting in $661 billion in sales. Furthermore, according to a recent *USA Today* article by Paul Davidson, the number of people employed by call centers throughout the United States is estimated to be close to 6.5 million. Call centers function in almost every industry, providing an extremely cost-effective way for conducting business. The telephone saves time and money for both customers and businesses. With all this business taking place, one big complaint can be heard again and again—the lack of customer service in the call center environment.

Our focus here is customer service from a call center perspective. We believe that while call centers are potentially the perfect environment for role-model customer service, this is usually not the case. A call center, in one form or another, represents a business that provides or is willing to provide a service. Even if the actual work is outsourced, the call center is acting on behalf of a business and therefore acting as its agent. The bottom line is that customers see the call center as "The Business."

With the national Do Not Call Registry now in effect, building revenue on different fronts will become even more critical for businesses. In addition to identifying and exploiting up-selling and cross-selling opportunities through savvy analysis of a customer's current situation and questioning, companies will have to focus on how they service customers to keep them coming back. Most customers who take their business elsewhere do so because a company fails to provide something that's very important—good service. Super service is part of filling this income gap.

Looking at the different kinds of call centers, we see that they generally fall into two major categories: inbound and outbound. A call center's audience may be either other businesses (business to business) or consumers (business to consumer). Call centers facilitate a number of activities including: sales, customer service, support, technical assistance, order fulfillment, collections, data gathering, and satisfaction surveys just to name a few.

Having run an outbound business to business call center since 1991, we are intimately aware of a call center's link between each customer and The Business. Our customers are the businesses that engage us to make calls on their behalf. Yet indirectly the people in the business we call are also our customers as well. Beyond our own outbound center, we have experience working within an inbound support center in an information technology environment as well as an outbound telemarketing center for a large telecommunication company. As business owners and consumers ourselves, we are both prospects who receive calls and customers who place calls to purchase goods/services or obtain assistance.

We personally believe that a call center has the opportunity to not only provide service to a company but to create long-term, loyal customers. Customer service at its best ensures a pleasant, successful experience attracting a customer's return business; at its worst, it not only loses a customer but also ensures that the lost customer will share his unhappiness with others. This is not the kind of recognition or branding any business wants. (For our purposes in this chapter, the word "customer" will refer to both prospects and customers that call center staff speak with.)

Within a call center, you do not have the luxury of *seeing* your customer. In many ways, you are blinded by your inability to pick up on and directly respond to the visual cues a customer provides during any interaction. Without your eyes, you have only your ears, openness to the emotions of others and your questioning techniques to ascertain where a person is coming from. Using your critical thinking skills, with the information you gather, you can develop a meaningful connection with your customer.

Your connection starts with the first contact. You are about to begin a relationship. Your ability to build this relationship is based on the language you use, your tone of voice, pleasing personality and critical-thinking skills. Moving forward, you can build the rapport you need to meet the expectations of and solve the concerns of your customers.

The heart of outstanding customer service starts with what we call the Behavior Model, illustrated in Figure #1 below.

THE BEHAVIOR MODEL

Illustration #1

In examining the Behavior Model, we see that the outer circle is Knowledge. Knowledge is the sum of all of our experience, learning and education. We collect and store more knowledge than will ever be directly useful to us. In fact, the key is being able to access useful knowledge when we need it. High performers retain the useful knowledge they need at the ready, which keeps them at the top of their game.

The second circle is Skill. Skill is the ability to effectively and productively use the knowledge we have. Barriers to skill development include:

- Lack of comfort with a new skill
- The stress of change – status quo is always easier
- Negative feedback

The third circle is Behavior. To effectively make a behavioral change, you have to practice and experience the change and be willing to push through any challenges or difficulties you might face. Success comes from successful behavior.

The Behavior Model comes to life regularly during any given work day, especially when dealing with an upset or demanding customer. You possess the knowledge, and you practiced the necessary skills. Now are you willing to exhibit the behavior that best fits the situation at hand?

In our call center, we use two methodologies to keep our customer service at the forefront of everything we do. First we use GO for BROKE which focuses on the behaviors an agent must exhibit in order to be successful. Secondly, we use Be a Customer CHAMPION. The simple truth is if you want your customers to keep coming back you must champion them.

All the same, none of what we discuss in this chapter would be of any value unless the principles of Valuing Customers and being a Customer Advocate were in place. Let's investigate what Valuing Customers and being a Customer Advocate is all about.

Valuing Customers

Customers are often called the lifeblood of an organization. The fact is that if it weren't for our customers, we wouldn't be here. Yet in working to do a good job, we can forget the simple fact that our customers provide our paychecks.

Customers respond to us based on their experiences with us. Did they have quality experiences? Did we understand and meet their needs? Did we focus on partnering and building relationships? Did we put our customers at ease?

A valued customer will return because of his or her experience with us. The fact is that sixty-eight percent of customers stop doing business with a company because of poor service. Studies also show that ninety percent of customers who cease doing business with a company make no effort to tell the firm why. (American Management Association)

In valuing our customers, we are always looking for new ways to enhance our relationships, improve awareness of our customers' needs, and ensure good communication. Just as you can identify a false smile, your customer knows if you care about her business. In this regard, our values, the fundamental guidelines we live our lives by, do determine how the world perceives us.

Customer Advocate

Working in a call center ultimately means you are both customer advocate and a company representative. Whether handling an inbound or outbound call, you are interacting with a customer who may or may not be an expert in this arena. Your responsibility is to assist the customer by providing him with the best information available allowing him to make an informed decision. In this way, you can use your experience and knowledge to make every interaction a successful one. As discussed earlier, this means you must know your product/service as well as know where to obtain additional information as you need it.

An integral part of being a customer advocate is customer focus. The first step here is to know who your customer is. Sometimes this may be more complicated than it appears. There may be several customers, not just one. They may be internal or they may be external.

Through understanding who your customers are, you can then understand their point of view. One of the most important customer focus skills is empathy—simply put, being able to put yourself in your customer's shoes. An old saying states, "People don't care how much you know until they know how much you care." Being able to see the situation through your customer's eyes will go a long way toward building a successful relationship between you and your customer. In this way, you identify solutions and solve problems through the unique perspective of the customer.

In everything you do, every choice you make, every action you take, the customer and the public see you as The Business. Your choices (how you handle yourself, your responses to others) will be pretty clear if you think of The Business as your company and always have in mind the way you would want others to see your company.

Remember that since you are The Business, you have the potential to bring new business in or to drive business away. All your actions should be positive, and your interactions with others should focus on a win-win outcome.

With the principles for Valuing Customers and being a Customer Advocate in place, it is time to explore the two methodologies for outstanding call center customer service. We will start with GO for BROKE which looks at individual behaviors you can develop to lead the field in customer service. Next we will delve into the Be a Customer CHAMPION methodology. Now, let's GO for BROKE.

GO for BROKE

With the Behavior Model in mind, let's look at what we need to do to provide excellent customer service. There are seven basic principles for excellent customer service in a call center. They are illustrated by the acrostic "GO for BROKE," a methodology taught in ADI Performance's **Prospecting for Sales Results** program. GO for BROKE requires more than just picking up a phone, getting a dial tone and dialing a number. GO for BROKE is the foundation for establishing successful habits, along with the ability to execute under all circumstances.

Many years ago, Professor Neil Smith shared with me a priceless piece of wisdom when he said, "It doesn't matter how hard you work unless you meet the standard." Working hard is not enough; you must also provide something of value. Many people work hard, yet they never slow down to determine how they can work better. At times, they get frustrated at the system yet do not apply themselves to excellence in what they do. GO for BROKE moves beyond working hard to working smart. Let's get started.

G - Get focused.

Being focused on what you are doing and when you are doing it is the first step to success. Focus is the one attribute that separates the few from the many. In a call center, agents must regularly deal with rejection and customer complaints. How you deal with these challenges will determine how successful you are. Beware of negative individuals. They will pull and drain your energy in an attempt to get you on their level, a level of anger, negativity, frustration, resentment and rejection. At this level, no one wins. You can take any negative situation and turn it into a win-win using the techniques outlined in the following pages. Keep any rejection you experience in perspective. Your focus is to represent the business in the best way possible. Staying focused on the positive outcomes you can achieve delivers positive outcomes.

Another part of focus is proper planning. Decide ahead of time what the purpose of the call will be. What do you want to get out of this call? Establish a relationship? Make a sale? Generate add-on business? What information do you need in order to meet your goal? Choose questions and behaviors that support that purpose.

While you are creating a plan for the call, mentally prepare yourself. Mental preparation and the right attitude are key factors when making the distinction between success and failure. Bringing a fresh, rested mind, well-versed in your product or service and infused with enthusiasm for each call, increases your chances of success.

O - Opportunity is everywhere.

Look around. No matter what the economic climate is, no matter how much people complain, there is opportunity all around you. Business is still taking place, and success stories are everywhere. Unfortunately, people spend too much time listening to negative input, like the news, or associating with naysayers. Find the good news, spend time with success-minded people, and be persistent; opportunities will start appearing. When opportunities for you appear, what will you do? Will you be ready to take advantage of them? Will you go after them? If you do not invest the energy to go after and develop them, they will disappear, lost forever in the vast ocean of opportunities passed by.

Where opportunity is concerned, having a positive attitude is an intangible that can give you an edge. Maintaining a positive approach is energizing and keeps you ready for new challenges. It shows in your thoughts, words, emotions, expression and posture. With a good attitude, you are also in the perfect position to be open to new ideas, exposing yourself to all kinds of philosophies and people. Being knowledgeable on many subjects increases your versatility. Clearly, part of being positive is a willingness to change, persevere and help others. Employing tact, common courtesies, sincerity, tolerance, humor, hope and patience makes working with others, whether fellow employees or customers, pleasant and fulfilling.

B - Believe in yourself and your product or service.

When initially speaking with someone on the phone, remember that you are viewed as the product or service. You are the first contact with the customer. Imagine that all the customer knows about your company is based on what you say and how you come across. Goodwill is yours to build or destroy. Now that is power! Your confidence in yourself and your product or service will come through in the way you choose and deliver your words. If you have no faith in what you are doing, how can the customer? You have the potential to be the absolute best in your field; the question is, "Do you believe it?"

There are no secrets to self-confidence. Knowing your stuff develops self-confidence. When you dedicate yourself, your time and energy to learning and being proficient at what you do, self-confidence is a natural byproduct. Believing in your skills and talents comes from mastering the basics and builds from there. However, if the fundamentals are not mastered, you will always be at a disadvantage. You will be unable to build if your foundation is not on a solid footing.

Product/service confidence comes from curiosity; a curiosity that drives you to know as much as you can about your company and its offerings. Understanding your connection with the customer and how to guide him or her through your own organization is important. You know you have the self-confidence you need when you pick up the phone and effectively handle an unpleasant and upset customer.

R - Review your communication habits.

What are your communication habits like? Do you speak clearly? Do you choose words that paint a picture? Are you speaking at a pace that allows the listener time to process and understand the message? Are you a good listener?

Working on the phone, your voice is your main tool. When someone hears your voice, he or she is developing a mental picture of who you are—your age, education level, believability and much more. To be understood, one must speak clearly. Clarity is accomplished through the different elements that make up vocal power. Some of the essential elements of vocal power are:

Diction—Clearly articulating and enunciating the words you use. Practice your diction by making sure that you hit all of the speech sounds contained in a word. When you run sounds together or leave end letters off words, you reduce clarity and also, potentially, your credibility.

Resonance—Provides a richness to the words you speak, making your message easier to understand.

Projection—Ensures that your voice can be clearly heard, so that you are neither too soft nor too overpowering.

Intonation—Provides emphasis and meaning to the words you are using. Change of pitch can entirely change a message. Proper intonation ensures you are conveying the appropriate message.

Pace—Your tempo animates your message. As your pace changes, so will the highs and lows (energy) in your voice.

Now that we've covered the elements of voice, let's look at how to make the words we chose work for us.

Words can either refine or confuse your message. Make sure the words you use fit the message you want to communicate and are appropriate for your customer. Use simple, common terms, avoiding acronyms and jargon that might be confusing. Selecting the right combination of words is not always as easy as it sounds. The English language is a rich language and provides us with many words to express what we want to say. The words you choose can be powerful or pitiful. Practice describing scenes around you. Choose words that paint vivid pictures and that attract the listener's interest. Thinking about the words you use and practicing how you put your words together, will put the power of the English language at your disposal.

Communication is not a one-way street, although many of us may act like it is. Vocal power and word selection are outbound communication vehicles. To make communication a two-way street, we must add listening. Listening is an art. Most of us love to talk but find active listening to be a challenge. Rather than truly engaging when someone is talking, we disengage and start to plan what we are going to say next or are distracted by one of the many barriers to good listening. Some barriers we must deal with include noise, closemindedness, impatience and imposed preconceptions.

Listening means staying focused and emotionally engaged when someone is communicating with you. This will build rapport and often provide you with the data you need to identify opportunities and solve problems. Listening also demonstrates that you care about what the speaker has to say. Your caring will build trust, allowing you to more quickly move into solution generation. At the same time, listening effectively, especially in a call center environment, requires objectivity on the part of the listener. Good listening builds cooperation and avoids errors, omissions and misunderstandings, which cost businesses millions of dollars every year.

O - Open the call with a winning statement.

Do you start every call with a winning statement? With an outbound call you only have about fifteen seconds to grab the listener, so craft your opening statement carefully. When handling inbound calls, your opening statement can help set the tempo for the call. Choose words that are intriguing and pique curiosity. Be engaging. Sound confident and enthusiastic. Create a statement that makes the listener want to know more. Grab them!

Whether making or accepting a call, you must sound confident and enthusiastic. You don't want to stumble over words, so decide what you will say and practice it with friends or in front of a mirror. Tape yourself and listen to how you sound. Are the words engaging? Is the voice smooth and confident? Does your enthusiasm shine through? If not, keep practicing!

When receiving an inbound call, forge a welcoming opening that lets the listener know you are there to provide impeccable service. Create a unique message.

In our society, one of the first opportunities you have to establish rapport is your greeting. An in-person greeting consists of making eye contact, smiling, approaching and extending your hand for a handshake with a verbal greeting. On the phone, we are missing most of these cues. What remains to us in our efforts to build rapport, are our voice, which is 84% of our message, and the words we choose, which is 16% of our message.

K - Know your product or service inside out.

You must be an expert on your product or service. Failure to answer questions or hesitancy in recommendations may cost you the customer's confidence. Do your homework. Study your discussion guide until you are completely versed in the product or service. Get someone to play "stump the telemarketer" with you. Get them to ask you questions about the product or service, looking for the unusual or difficult details. Practice until you can't be stumped. This will also help you improve your discussion guide.

E - Enthusiastically maintain confidence about yourself and your product or service.

Enthusiasm counts! Building on your great opening statement, delivered with enthusiasm and confidence, you can leverage this energy level throughout the conversation. You must be enthusiastic about yourself and your product. If you are tired, unsure, worried or, worse, don't care about the product or service you are selling, it will come through in your voice. Make sure you are mentally and physically ready to be enthusiastic and energetic throughout the conversation. Try some tongue twisters to warm up your voice and enunciation. And always remember your smile. A smile indicates a willingness to be approached, an openness. Smiles can be heard on the other end of your call.

If your product or service is you, present yourself in the best light possible.

GO for BROKE Worksheet

Below are activities that will help you deliver better customer service. Exercises and questions are designed to work on the knowledge, skills, and behavior you need to be successful.

Get Focused—List all the things that distract you when you are on the phone. Once you complete this list, go back and review it. Write down what you can do to eliminate or minimize the distractions. Next, take action on the ones you can control, and solicit assistance when needed.

Opportunity is Everywhere—Look around your environment. What skills do you possess or can you acquire that will make you a more valued employee? How do you build relationships that will help you within the business? What needs to be done to enhance the customer's perception of the business?

Believe in Yourself and Your Product or Service—Describe the value that you bring to your customers. How do you quantify that value?

Review Your Communication Habits—Locate some tongue twisters and practice them. Practice deep breathing. Write down a simple sentence, place the emphasis on different words, and hear how the meaning changes. Develop correct posture while in your chair. Develop listening skills by focusing on the speaker and managing listening barriers.

Open the Call with a Winning Statement—Write down your opening message. Practice with a tape recorder or a friend. Regularly revise and update your opening message to keep it fresh and up to date.

Know Your Product or Service Inside Out—Find the most knowledgeable person on the product or service. Ask him/her where you can find more information and if he/she will quiz you to test your knowledge. This will demonstrate your commitment to this coaching process. Most people love to help people who are willing to help themselves.

Enthusiastically Maintain Confidence about Yourself and Your Product or Service—List what causes you to lose your enthusiasm and confidence. Once identified, develop a strategy to counter those enemies when they appear.

GO for BROKE has shown us how to position ourselves to excel at delivering excellent customer service no matter what business we are in, how to overcome the obstacles in front of us and how to see our job and our customers in a new light. Next we will dig into Be a Customer CHAMPION which is all about what you do on behalf of the relationship you want to nurture and grow with each customer you touch. Understanding and incorporating into your approach, the essentials of championing your customer will separate you from the crowd, putting you at the top of your game.

C - Creatively use your resources.

No business has unlimited resources. In fact, the competitive advantage rests in how resources are utilized. Your competitors are striving to maximize their resources. Your creativity in resource management is a major contributor to your organization's growth.

If you want to be able to make the best decisions for you, your customer and the business, critical-thinking skills are required. Each day, employees make numerous decisions that affect performance and the overall quality and quantity of work produced by the company. Three major factors that demonstrate the effectiveness of each employee are the employee's knowledge of his/her job, the employee's relationship with others and the employee's attitude or emotional state.

Job performance increases with enhanced thinking skills. Critical thinking provides a fundamental methodology to look at one job function and identify where improvements can be made. In today's work environment, with the mantra of doing more with less, being able to see clearly how performance can be done faster, better, cheaper or not at all is the difference between success and failure.

H - Have respect for yourself and your customer.

Respect comes from your attitude, how you carry yourself and the image you project. Individuals with positive attitudes are most likely to think in the best interest of the customer and the business. Individuals with negative attitudes tend not to think in those terms. The consequences of attitude are always present but may be difficult to identify. Having a professional image and a positive attitude goes a long way to building customer relationships. Remember, the reason that seventy percent of customers go elsewhere has nothing to do with the product:

Twenty percent switch because they have too little contact and personal attention.

Fifty percent switch because the attention received was rude and unhelpful.

You have a tremendous impact on how the customer feels about The Business. Your behavior can make the difference in whether or not the customer chooses to buy from The Business or elsewhere.

A - Apply the power of questions.

Need an answer? Ask a question! Questions help us find our way when lost, make better decisions, change lives, improve processes, save lives and decide what to have for dinner. Questions are some of the most powerful tools we have.

For most of us, having the correct information is essential to doing a good job. Often, all the necessary information we need doesn't just present itself. We must seek it out. That's where questioning come in.

189

There are two forms of questioning that we can use—open and closed. Open questions encourage the sharing of information in a free-flowing manner. Through careful listening, you will discover and understand data you were not expecting, or your assumptions about a situation might be challenged. It is important to be prepared to handle the information you receive, to adapt and adjust to new circumstances.

Sometimes, we ask an open question and are overwhelmed with the information that comes back to us. For example, when you ask the question, "How are you?" you usually expect to hear, "Fine. And you?" What happens when the person asked really tells you how they are? You know, "My back hurts. My car broke down. My daughter's in a school play, and I have to get there this afternoon without the car. My boss is expecting this report before I leave. I had to make coffee this morning, because some idiot took the last cup and forgot to make a new pot. It's my turn to do the icebreaker at the staff meeting, and I don't feel like breaking ice. My dog bit the neighbor down the street, and now they are suing me." Is that enough information for you? More than enough! So we use open questions to gather lots of information.

The other kind of question we use is a closed question. Closed questions are used to gather specific information. Some examples of closed questions are, "What is your name?" "How long has the service been out?" "What is the name of your service provider?" "What is your address?" "What is your phone number?" "Where is the product being shipped?" These questions are not designed to elicit a lot of information but rather limited, targeted facts.

You may be wondering, "What does this mean to me, my job and my ability to service the customer?" (Note that this is an open question designed to elicit a lot of information.) In order to do the job and provide good service to the customer, you need to have sufficient information to make good decisions and act in the best interest of the customer.

Think about using the basic journalism questions as a foundation for your information gathering. Those basic questions are who, what, why, when, where and how. Let's look at how these six simple questions can help you to successfully serve the customer.

Who?—Who is the customer? The more you know about who is involved, the better you can interact with the appropriate people.

What?—What are we doing? What do I know? What don't I know? (This is a powerful question! What you don't know can trip you up.) What is the goal? What are the objectives? What is the budget? What are the advantages of doing it this way? What is the down side? What will it take to achieve customer satisfaction? What did we do well? What could we have done better? It is essential for you to have a clear and common understanding of the what (the goal).

Why?—Why am I here? Why did the customer call us? Why is this customer frustrated? Why are we doing this job, in this way, with these tools? Why did we choose these methods? Understanding the why can help you see the big picture. Once you understand the big picture, you can move on to the other questions and collect some details.

Where?—Where is the problem? Where is the product/service needed? Where are you located? Where are the resources I need? Knowing the answer to "Where?" can save you a lot of time and aggravation. When you know where all the equipment/tools/people are, you don't have to waste time looking for them.

When?—When did the problem first occur? When would be the best time for me to get in touch with you? When will payment be made? When would you like to meet? Knowing the when helps you to develop a timeline for your project.

How?—How long has the problem existed? How can we fix it? How could we make it better? How could we improve the product/service? The how question helps us to come up with new ways and to improve on old ones.

We ask questions, and we receive answers. Do we know everything now? No. You may know all that is possible to know at that given moment, yet you should never stop asking questions and gathering information. The more information you have, the better.

Let's look at five areas where questioning is a powerful tool:

Obtains and clarifies information

We receive massive amounts of information all day long, both on the job and in our personal lives. On the job, we often find ourselves handling a customer request, a co-worker's need for assistance or our boss giving a job assignment. Often, we do not get all the information we need during our interactions. We may not be focused on the matter at hand, or perhaps we are distracted by outside elements. Obtaining accurate information and a clear understanding of circumstances will always save you time and help you avoid errors. It is important to stop for a minute and ensure understanding of the important messages you receive.

Provokes thought

Have you ever been in a conversation where a question or comment made you stop and think? You realize you have never thought of something in that way. You just gained new insight! It may or may not change the way you think about something, but at the very least, it gives you a different perspective. Sometimes, you are asked a question that gives you a great deal to think about.

Provides control in a situation

Questions are a powerful tool to control a situation. In fact, if used correctly, they provide you and others with a better understanding of a situation. By asking the right questions, you can obtain information that will assist in shaping your strategy for dealing with conflict. In fact, asking the right questions can help diffuse tense situations. Once you clearly understand the other person's point of view, you can move more quickly to a win-win position.

Promotes the power of persuasion

The best way to get someone to see things from your point of view is through questions. We all have our own opinions. However, we may not have all the facts. If you can determine a person's perspective through questions, you can better ask questions to provide a different perspective. In fact, your audience may persuade themselves.

Helps us to listen better

When we ask a question, we have a self-interest in hearing the answer. Learning the art of effective questioning assists us in becoming better listeners. If we do not listen effectively, the advantage questions provide us will be diminished. We have to listen to others to obtain true understanding. You will see improved relationships with your customers, fellow employees, management and those in your personal life. That is quite an incentive to improve your listening and questioning skills!

M - Make time to really listen.

There is no substitute for good listening. It makes the conveyor of the message feel valued. Good listening reduces mistakes and at the same time builds solid business relationships. Develop and implement an action plan to improve this vital communication skill.

First, listen to the customer. If you use active listening skills and demonstrate empathy, your customer will be more willing to listen to you. For example, a customer is upset with a bill she has received and is calling you. Rather then trying to explain the process (which the customer could care less about), listen, acknowledge what her complaint is and let her know you can understand how she could feel that way. You are not agreeing with her but rather expressing understanding. Remember, we have all been upset as consumers at one point or another. If you let her vent, for example, she will calm down more quickly. Once she knows you are not fighting her or explaining how the company is right, she is more likely to listen to you.

P - Promptly respond to concerns.

When customers share their concerns with you, it is your responsibility to act. It is critical to business success that you do so. We would all like to give the customer good news; however, no matter whether it's good or bad, the information must be provided as quickly as possible and in a professional manner. In a call center, you are at a distinct disadvantage since the customer feels protected by distance and you cannot recognize her.

There's a saying that suggests you do not know whether or not you have a customer until a problem occurs. That's right; you need a problem to solidify customer loyalty. If you want loyal customers, you have to provide a service when they really need it, which is usually when they have a problem.

Being on the front line working with customers, one of your responsibilities is to successfully manage challenging and angry customers. So what do you do when things go wrong? The answer is to *think*, remaining in control when a challenge comes your way.

When any problem comes your way, be sure you understand the situation and take a few moments to analyze it. During this process, try to get the whole picture, not just your point of view. There is almost always another way to do everything. Consider all your alternatives before you take action. What is the best move for the customer? What will best meet his/her needs and concerns?

Implement the "No Excuses" rule.

Never tell a customer what you can't do; only tell him what you can do. I cannot emphasize strongly enough that telling a customer what can't be done is adding fuel to the fire. For example, let's say a customer is calling you because he wants something or has a problem. Rather than saying there is nothing you can do about it, you could document the problem and tell the customer how it will be followed up on and handled.

The reality is that your customer doesn't want to know what you can't do. Focus your answers and actions on what you can do. Think "positive action," and make it something in your control. Don't blame others, even if it is their fault. Focus on what you and The Business are doing to make the situation right.

Offer win-win solutions.

We must understand both our customers and our needs. Talking win-win is easy. The actual practice is more difficult. We are surrounded by win-lose activities, including business competition, political elections and sporting events, just to mention a few. We must stay focused on the desired outcome and not remain attached to our personal outcome. We need to be mentally prepared to enter into a win-win agreement. If we take advantage of someone, we have violated basic relationship principles, and there will be consequences. Unexpressed feelings never die, and you will receive a payback, normally at the most inopportune time.

When you choose an alternative, own it. Whatever the outcome, you made the best choice you could based on the information you had at the time. Don't second guess yourself.

Nurture customer relationships.

Imagine your best customer experience and give it to each customer you interface with. There are many instances when we may respond to others according to how we perceive them. Imagine every customer as an excellent customer and treat him/her that way. Odds are, sooner or later, he/she will respond to you in like manner.

Always keep your customer's expectations at the forefront of your mind. This will tell you what direction to move in. Keep your focus on the customer, and make your decision using your organizational values.

Success in customer service comes from exhibiting behaviors that build rapport, listening and taking positive action.

When we do each of the things outlined in this chapter, we create winning opportunities for ourselves and others. The long-term goal is to work each of these skills until it becomes part of our behaviors. That is, we don't have to think about what comes next; instead, we take action using the skills we've developed. The natural byproduct is great customer service, with you as the champion.

James R. Dawson and Jennifer M. Dawson

 Jim Dawson is an entertaining speaker, highly effective trainer, and experienced performance coach who uses innovative sharing and hands-on techniques to help individuals strengthen their communication and customer service skills. Working with clients from a variety of industries and roles, Jim easily creates an energized learning environment that captivates audiences, provokes thought, and inspires action. He is dedicated to helping every client realize a greater sense of self-expectation and new levels of performance that lead to expanded career options and a more satisfying work/life balance. Currently responsible for customer operations for both ADI Performance and ADI Marketing, Jennifer Dawson is highly experienced in helping organizations build superior customer service teams that enhance bottom-line results. Her strengths include developing and deploying customer-focused strategies that form the foundation and infrastructure for managed organizational growth and profitability. Instituting project management systems; improving hiring, development, and training practices; and employing customer-friendly processes are just a few of the ways she has helped professionals and organizations expand their market presence and build long-term client relationships. Jim and Jennifer are not only business partners; they are a dynamic father-daughter team passionate about helping their clients achieve "Go for Broke" customer service.

James R. Dawson
Jennifer M. Dawson
Managing Partners, ADI Performance
P.O. Box 70083
Marietta, GA 30007
770.640.0840 office
800.234.1550 toll free
770.594.0567 fax
e-mail: jrdawson@adiperformance.com
e-mail: jmdawson@adiperformance.com
website: www.adiperformance.com

Chapter Eleven

Customer Service And The Plane Ride From Hell

Peter Quinones

Few subjects in business are as daunting as customer service. Likewise, few are so rewarding and, ultimately, worthy of study. So vast is the amount of work in existence on the topic—books, articles, audio and visual programs, online courses, live courses—that one feels a bit humbled by it all. It's hard to know what else can be contributed to the tremendous body of knowledge that we already have. What we do know, though, is that poor and mediocre service is everywhere, all around us, every day, in virtually every aspect of our lives. Who's never gotten transferred into voice mail hell in the course of a phone call? Have you ever had the pleasure of being waited on by an inattentive, bored, half-asleep server at a restaurant? Have you ever had a clerk in a store keep you waiting for an eternity while she chatted on the phone? Here's an old favorite: The sofa you ordered was supposed to arrive at your door two weeks after the date of purchase, and a month later, it's still not delivered, and the store doesn't return your calls.

Sadly, these kinds of things go on all the time in every sort of business transaction imaginable. This isn't to say that there aren't purchase experiences or business transactions that aren't rewarding or even downright joyous. Of course, there are. These are great when they happen, and they do a lot to reaffirm our faith in humanity when they do, because they make us feel so good. I believe, however, that most of our experiences as customers and potential customers lie between the extremes and can be categorized as just so-so.

This realization—the recognition of most of our experiences as customers being only fair—has been explained recently by Jeffrey Gitomer and others. It is the fallacy of "customer satisfaction," the idea that businesses should be shooting for satisfaction as opposed to loyalty. We'll be looking at this idea a little more closely later on.

In this chapter, we'll be examining seven significant customer service concepts. Three of these are orthodox principles of customer service. I call them orthodox, because they appear to be universal fundamentals that pop up in one form or another, under one name or another, in virtually every customer service system I've seen, read about or studied. The principles are 1) Exceed the customer's expectations, 2) Put out fires, and overcompensate for mistakes and 3) Strive for customer satisfaction.

These sacrosanct principles are, of course, time tested and valuable. They work. While I wouldn't claim that they are the only eternal principles of customer service, they seem to be included in most systems and are the ones I believe to be most easily identifiable and readily available for examination.

In addition to these three orthodox ideas, we'll look at four more concepts that come from outside the area of business proper. These are the Veil of Ignorance, the Message vs. the Metamessage, The Slide and Preemption.

Once we've looked at these seven ideas and gotten a little background on them, we can take a look at a story that illustrates violations of many of the principles of good customer service and see how they could have been avoided.

1. Exceed Expectations

In my readings, I've come across many books that dwell in great length on the subject of exceeding a customer's expectations in a transaction, of going way above and beyond the call of duty in order to serve a customer well and provide that "Wow!" type of experience. One such book is *Positively Outrageous Service* by T. Scott Gross. Another is *The Nordstrom Way* by Robert Spector and Patrick McCarthy, and a third is *The Pursuit of Wow!* by Tom Peters. All of these illustrate the same basic point: If you want people to remember you, if you want them to keep coming back to you and refer other business your way, and if you want to differentiate yourself in your customers' minds, then you must give them a little more than they believe they've paid for.

Here's an example. You pull up to the drive-through window at a fast-food place. While you wait on line to order, someone appears with a cloth and Windex and proceeds to clean your windshield and windows. Wow! Pretty amazing. Service like that is totally unexpected, rarely seen anywhere and way beyond expectations. Chances are that once you get service like that, you'll be going back again and again, right? You'll also probably tell all your friends, who will probably tell their friends, etc. Experiences of this kind are so rare that they virtually ensure large amounts of word-of-mouth business.

In my own experience as an eBay seller, I have managed to keep my feedback rating at a perfect one hundred percent by exceeding expectations in all kinds of ways. First, I ship the items to my winning bidders as soon as the auction ends, whether they have paid me yet or not. It seems that most sellers will absolutely not ship an order until they have been paid, but by working on the honor system, I've shown people that they can trust me, because I trust them. Another thing I'll do is include a small bonus item or gift in with the order. Since my prices are already super competitive, people really feel that they're getting a deal with me. I go out of my way to e-mail my customers the tracking number of the item so they can check the progress of their orders online or by phone. While these three actions are assuredly no big deal, most people seem to appreciate them enormously. Judging by the comments I get from buyers, hardly any other sellers do any of these things, so when I do them for people, it exceeds their expectations by a mile. I once had a buyer tell me a story about a seller who claimed to have sent her a package. She never got it. She asked him to provide a tracking number so she could flag the order down, and he responded that he had just mailed it plain old parcel post and had no tracking number. He claimed that wasn't his responsibility. She asked what he planned to do about the situation, and he said he wasn't planning to do anything! His position was that he had fulfilled all his obligations to her whether she had gotten the package or not! Incredible! How would you like to do business with this guy?

Both of these examples show how a business can go way beyond expectations and keep the customer happy and wanting to do business again and again. Remember that people are so conditioned to poor and mediocre service that if their expectations are exceeded, even by just a little bit, it stands out big time.

One note: While exceeding expectations is a great strategy, relying on it exclusively may not be the wisest course. It forces you to be in a constant, neverending, creative mode. Why do I say that? Because if you have a method of exceeding expectations that works and you have astute competitors, they'll copy it, and you'll thus lose your originality and competitive advantage. You'll then have to think of something else. Of course, they'll copy that also, and so on and so on. Just think of things like frequent flyer miles or loaner cars, and you'll have an idea of how something that once uniquely exceeded customers' expectations was copied by everyone in the given industry until it became a hygiene factor instead of a service novelty; it became standard practice. Any innovative "exceed expectations" strategy will eventually be in the same boat.

2. Put Out Fires

Let's face it: We all make mistakes, and sometimes, we make big ones. In business, as in any other part of life, we feel the need to make up for the blunder. Of course, in business, we have the added risk of losing customers and money. Customers develop a real sick feeling when businesses screw up. At an intuitive level, we all understand this desire to rectify a mistake and make good, but let's look at a few examples.

You dash into a restaurant for a quick take-out order at lunchtime—a chicken sandwich. You get back to your office and discover that it's a steak sandwich! Annoyed, inconvenienced and hungry, you bring it back. To your delight, they not only correct the error but throw in a free desert and give you a gift certificate to come back for dinner with your family, on the house. Wow! Not only did the restaurant put out the fire caused by their initial mistake but they went out of their way to show sincerity and caring by overcompensating with the free dinner.

In their book *A Complaint Is A Gift*, the authors Janelle Barlow and Claus Moller show us how recognizing a problem and moving to correct it immediately can be just as effective as if everything went perfectly in the first place. They give several examples: a brand new sweater shrinks in its first wash; the trunk of a just-purchased car doesn't close correctly; a turkey that a customer bought for Thanksgiving dinner doesn't have any giblets. In each of these instances, the customer is actually giving the business the chance to compensate, to make up for the problem, to get things right and thus demonstrate that they sincerely care. Unfortunately, claim the authors, in most cases like these, the service rep completely misunderstands the deeper, underlying message and will start to fight or argue with the customer.

What is this underlying message? In each case, the customer is giving the business a chance to prove itself. They are, in effect, saying, "Take care of this problem and I will continue to be your customer." It would be very easy for the clothing store to say the customer didn't follow the washing instructions on the label, that the customer broke the latch on the trunk after he accepted the car or that the turkey must have had giblets. Barlow and Moller write that employees get defensive and feel that they are being blamed and thus move to shift the blame in these situations onto something else, be it company policy or whatever. This is where breakdown and miscommunication occur. In the above examples, if the customers' concerns are not addressed, there is almost no chance that they will do business with those companies again. However, if the fire is put out, the reverse is true; it is almost certain that the customers will become loyal advocates. Taking care should be viewed as a long-term investment rather than as a short-term loss.

The bottom line, then, is that we must be aware at all times of the opportunity to set things right for a customer when a situation has gone awry. The title of the book says it all: *A Complaint Is A Gift*.

3. Customer Satisfaction

Another book with a title that says it all is Jeffrey Gitomer's *Customer Satisfaction Is Worthless, Customer Loyalty Is Priceless*. The main premise of this book is that a satisfied customer is a lukewarm customer, one who will basically still shop around, whereas a loyal customer is a fanatic who wouldn't begin to think of bringing her business anywhere else. In particular, the kinds of customer satisfaction surveys that are so much in vogue these days are little more than "corporate butt-covering documents," to use Gitomer's hilarious phrase. They really don't mean a whole heck of a lot.

All they really do is confirm that everyone did his or her job in the minimally acceptable way. We've all seen these surveys in hotels or restaurants; we've all been mailed these surveys or called on the phone to do them. In my own personal experience, I've worked for organizations that put incredible emphasis on surveys of this kind, surveys that contained questions like, "How would you rate the purchase of your new X on a scale of one to five?" "How would you rate your salesperson?" "Would you do business with us again?" etc. Of course, none of this information does anything to help anybody in business achieve their true objective, which is to capture loyal customers. What makes matters worse is that in many organizations that use surveys of this type, the customer is basically confronted by a salesperson or sales manager with pleas such as, "Please give us a good rating on the survey when they call you," and in many cases, they'll do it just to make the salesperson go away. Their answers are not really indicative of anything.

I always get a chuckle when I see surveys of this kind in hotels, the little survey cards that say, "Please fill out and leave at front desk." Oh really! Suppose you make some disapproving comments or say something negative. Do you think that person at the front desk is going to zip that survey right over to corporate headquarters? Or is it going to go right into the trash? Let's be real!

A great question Gitomer asks is: "If I offered you 1,000 satisfied customers or 1,000 loyal customers, which would you rather have?" Isn't that a spectacular question? It immediately shows us why we should be going for loyalty through meaningful action rather than satisfaction through silly surveys.

Ultimately, the point is that these types of satisfaction surveys confuse a frozen moment in time—the point of purchase—with the entire ownership experience, which we all know can stretch out for months or years. In order to get a truly representational picture, you would have to survey the customer at regular intervals during the entire period of ownership. This, of course, is something that all top salespeople, if not their organizations, do all the time; they stay in touch throughout the years and months. In my automotive selling career, I've had people who got a postcard from me every month for five or six years. True, they always called me if they had a problem, but they also always called me if they or a friend needed a new vehicle. In other words, they exemplified the rule, "Loyal is better than satisfied."

4. The Veil of Ignorance

In moving outside the orthodox now, we'll begin with a concept that comes from far outside the arena of business and business literature. This is known as the Veil of Ignorance, and it comes from the book *A Theory of Justice*, which was the major work of the seminal twentieth century philosopher John Rawls. It has been my observation that consistent implementation of this idea in business brings huge personal and financial rewards. So what is it all about?

Imagine that you are a disembodied spirit—a soul in heaven, if you will. Now you know that come tomorrow, you are about to enter the human world as a whole being, a soul inside some human body. You have no idea who you are going to be; you've been kept completely ignorant of that. You could literally be any human being who has ever lived, in any historical period, from the time that human beings still lived in caves right up to the present moment and any time in between. You could be the king of the land or the poorest person living in the gutter. You could be male or female or of any country, race, religion, social status, level of intelligence, degree of physical ability or disability, etc. You just don't know. You could be the same person that you are this very minute, or you could be an aborigine in the Australian Outback in 5,000 B.C. When you really stop and meditate on this idea for a few moments, it blows your mind, doesn't it?

One last thing: Immediately before you enter the realm of the human, you will be given the power to write the laws of the society that you are about to inhabit, and the laws that you write will be final. Everyone must obey them without question. You are creating the laws of the land.

What kind of laws will you write? Will you write laws that favor one group or kind of person over the others or at the expense of others, or will you write laws that are equally fair to everyone? Will you write a law, for example, denying women the power to vote? Would you write laws like those found in India's caste system, forbidding those who are born poor to ever get out of poverty? Remember, you could be in any one of these groups of people. Anything other than equal and fair laws could hurt you.

The answer to these and other examples we might think of is obviously no, because you yourself might be a member of the group that is hurt by these unjust rules. We would all try to write laws that were as fair as possible to everybody.

The Veil of Ignorance is the way in which you appear to view people. In serving customers, it means treating everyone the same, showing no prejudgment of what they may or may not buy or what their needs might be. Seeing this concept in action is the easiest way to understand it. Let's look at an example. I know a gentleman who now owns a sales training company, but in the late 1980s and early 1990s, he was working as a salesperson in a large Mercedes Benz dealership in New Jersey. On one particularly nasty winter day, there wasn't a lot of action in the showroom, and a young African

American gentleman in his early twenties happened in. You must remember that at this time, the rap lifestyle wasn't really a mainstream part of the culture yet; it was still a little bit on the periphery, and most of the salespeople in the place had obviously decided that this person was not a serious Mercedes Benz buyer. My salesman acquaintance, however, had his Veil of Ignorance ready and went up to the young man to see if he could answer any questions.

At first, the young man was hesitant to talk much and just kind of moved from car to car. Then he sat in an expensive convertible and asked the salesman, "Can we sit down and figure out how much I would have to bring you a check for if I wanted to buy this car, cash, tomorrow?" The salesman said, "Of course. Sure. We can do that," and they sat down at his desk and did the calculations. Immediately afterward, the young man gave him a credit card and told him to run a ten thousand dollar deposit. Admittedly a little skeptical, the salesman ran the charge, and it was approved! The next day the customer came back with a certified check and an insurance card and drove out with the car!

Who was he? As it happened, he was a relative of one of the rappers in a group that was becoming huge in the music industry at that time, and he worked as one of their managers. They were selling millions of records and were doing very well. As he was about to drive off in his new car, the young man said to the salesman, "You know, I must have gone to ten car dealerships, and you were the only person who even spoke to me. Thanks!"

Question: If he wasn't even in the group, and he bought a Mercedes, do you think the guys in the group also bought some? When they did, which salesman do you think they went to see? And when they bought cars for their family members? And when they talked to producers and other performers in the rap industry, which salesman did they recommend? Would you believe that this salesman traced probably fifty or sixty deals back to that first young man he helped? What kind of monetary compensation does a salesman get from selling sixty Mercedes Benz automobiles? And it all came from practicing the Veil of Ignorance, not prejudging anyone but assuming everyone is a potential customer and treating them with your best customer service. Implement this powerful practice, and the universe will respond!

5. Message vs. Metamessage

In linguistics, there is a concept called the "metamessage." This is the underlying message given by the way you communicate, by the surroundings and by everything else that you do. It can be very different from the message you literally say or write. The metamessage is implied, inferred and left unsaid. It could be physical or psychological, tangible or intangible. Here's a quick example: My friend asks me how I like her new haircut. I say, "Looks great!" Then, the following week, the birthday present I giver her is a gift certificate to a salon that cuts hair in a totally different style. The metamessage is, "Your hairstyle doesn't become you. Fix it."

Many times, I've sat down with a couple to discuss a car deal. I'll present them with a proposal, and the husband will look to the wife and ask, "What do you think?" The wife will shrug and say, "It's your car, honey." He'll look to me and say, "Okay, let's do it." I cringe! Ouch! Her message is yes, but what is she really telling him? What's the metamessage?

In your business, your metamessages are very strong, and they influence customers to no end. In their classic book *Customers For Life*, Carl Sewell and Paul Brown even devote a whole chapter to the care of your bathrooms! If even the condition of your bathroom can send a metamessage, what else in your business is speaking for you? Much of this is going on at a subconscious level, and customers may never consciously deliberate in the forefront of their consciousness why they don't want to do business with you, but they go elsewhere nonetheless.

My local supermarket sends out a very powerful, positive metamessage by several things it does. First, at strategic points all around the store, they have pictures of all the various managers on the walls. The produce manager is by the apples, the meat manager is at the butcher counter, the grocery manager is by the bread, etc. It's fun, because as you push your cart around the store, you identify the various people "in action, in living color," before your very eyes, working and helping customers. Another thing they do is hang the results of mystery shopping visits all around the store for you to observe. It shows that they take pride in their work and want to do a good job. As you pay, the cashiers are nice and friendly and always ask if you found everything you needed. The positive metamessages are everywhere. No wonder the place is full of shoppers twenty-four hours a day!

Contrast this with a local convenience store where the floors inside and the parking lot outside are always filthy, the workers are inattentive to your requests, and the checkout person snaps gum in her jaws and tells you, "Have a nice day" in a bored monotone while already looking over your shoulder toward the next customer. What kind of metamessage is that? Is it positive or negative? What kind of impact on the store's bottom line will there be?

Pay close attention to the metamessages that your people and your facilities are giving off; they provide you with very important clues and feedback about what your customers are thinking.

6. The Slide

The Slide occurs when you have a customer service problem, and you're quite aware of it, but no matter what you do to try and correct the problem, it just keeps getting worse, and you have to take very drastic measures or else rely on a bolt from the blue to intervene.

Sometimes a situation will slide out of control, and you will lose a customer, and there is absolutely nothing you can do about it. For example, airlines sometimes have to bump customers from flights. We all know this, and we all agree to it when we buy a ticket. But virtually no one is very understanding or happy when it happens, and periodically, an airline will lose a customer forever over a bump. It's just the nature of the business and cannot be avoided.

I once mailed a package to Tennessee. Two days later, checking the delivery confirmation online, I read that the package was being processed at a distribution center in upstate New York. How wonderful! When I called the help line to gain some insight, the gentleman told me, "This package is going to Florida!" When I asked how that could be, he said "The Zip code it's going to is 33, correct?" I told him no, that it was 37. He said that probably what had happened was the clerk had mistaken my seven for a three. "But how come on the online tracking it says the package is going to upstate New York?" I asked. He said he had no idea and began a three-way call between himself, me and a supervisor at the upstate New York post office. This person proceeded to tell us that the package was on its way to the national return center of a well-known department store! By the time I hung up the phone, my eyes were spinning.

The end of the story is fairly humorous. The following day, the person in Tennessee called me to let me know he had gotten the package. Wow! How crazy. You see what I mean when I say that sometimes you just have to rely on a bolt from the blue?

In another instance, I had a customer who had won a book in one of my eBay auctions. She sent an e-mail stating that she planned to pay by personal check, which was fine. Instead of waiting about a week to get the check in the mail and then another ten days for the check to clear, I shipped the book right away, in what I thought was a nice little customer service gesture. After two weeks, I hadn't heard from her, so I sent a little reminder and got no reply. I sent another reminder; again, no reply. The third time, I sent the official non-paying-buyer notice, and she immediately replied, "My sister-in-law handles my books." I replied that that was fine but didn't really explain why I hadn't been paid. She answered, "Are you sure? We assumed we had paid you, because we had the book." I said no, if she would kindly check her records, she would see that no check to me had been cashed. She asked, "Well, why would you send the book before you were paid? This is most unusual." I replied that it was just a friendly gesture to try and make customers happy. She queried, "Are you from America?" This went on and on. We finally got it straightened out, but it was obvious that my deviation from the usual pattern of events had upset her.

As you probably know, a big element of eBay auctions is the Feedback, in which buyers and sellers rate each other positively or negatively. I could tell that if I didn't do something to unruffle this customer's feathers, I might get a negative feedback, so I sent her a small book as a gift and a way of making up for the confusion, even though all the confusion was caused by her! In this manner, I stopped the situation from sliding out of control.

7. Preemption and a Plane Ride

The last concept we're going to take a look at is Preemption, which involves analyzing problems that may crop up in your business from time to time and arranging for effective responses ahead of time, way before the situation actually arises in real life.

We're going to look at a little story and then apply the idea of preemption to it. Some years back, I was taking a packed early-morning flight from California to New York. Every seat on the big 747 was taken except for the one that was right next to mine. I was in the very back of the plane in the seat that backs up to the wall and won't lean back. Everyone was buzzing with anticipation for the flight to start, for us to get in the air and get going. Fifteen minutes went by, thirty, forty-five, and we were still on the ground. Everyone wondered what was going on. Finally, we could hear a person being brought onto the plane who was quite angry, cursing, using profanity and threatening lawsuits. And boy, was he mad! His face was purple with rage.

I told you there was one empty seat on the plane, right? That's right, he sat right next to me and kept right on complaining, threatening and making rude remarks. Everyone in the area was a little nervous but glad that we were finally taking off. After a short time, we were up in the air, and my very upset neighbor started to doze off a bit. By the way, I eventually found out that the reason he was so upset was that he had been bumped off not just one but two earlier flights! Still, it seemed to me that he was so upset that he shouldn't have been on the plane, among innocent passengers, at all.

The flight attendants began to serve breakfast, and I noticed that after they got most of the way down the aisles they started counting. They counted the passengers in seats, and then they counted the breakfasts on the cart. One came over to me and whispered in a concerned tone, "I'm sorry sir, but there seems to have been a terrible mistake. We don't have enough breakfasts for everybody on the plane. We do have some leftover salad we can offer you." Salad! It was five o'clock in the morning! Anyway, you can imagine how my neighbor reacted to this news. He flipped out again! However, the flight attendant was able to eke out a muffin and a cup of coffee somewhere, and this pacified him a little bit. I didn't get any; I had to eat my salad!

My neighbor wasn't done, however. The flight attendants had (erroneously, in my opinion) assumed things were okay for the moment and had retired to the kitchen area, which was blocked off by a little curtain. My neighbor declared he wanted a glass of juice and jumped up, stormed over to the curtain and tore it open to reveal the attendants sitting in their private space—eating breakfast!

Well, if you think you know what the word "rage" means, you haven't seen anything yet! He went berserk, flailing about, punching, screaming, biting. There was complete and total chaos in the plane as the crew, with help from some passengers, tackled him and tied him up. I don't know where they took him for the remainder of the flight— maybe down with the luggage—but it was a very scary experience!

There are so many examples of poor customer service in this story. It's a virtual course on what not to do. Many of the ideas and concepts we've discussed here can be found, and it would be quite worthwhile to try and identify opportunities for their implementation one by one. Let's look at what an example preemption chart might look like as we identify possible problems and solutions for each:

Preemption: Plane
Problem: The customer must be bumped.
Solution: Bump him a second time. (Just kidding!)
Solution: Get him on another flight ASAP, even if it means getting him on a competing airline.

Problem: There are no tickets available on any airline.
Solution: Determine if there are any flights to the same destination at any airport within a reasonable driving or flying distance, or if there is even a connecting flight leaving from any such airport.

Problem: There are no flights from anywhere in the vicinity.
Solution: Find out why it is so important he fly out right away – is he delivering something, or meeting somebody? Can anyone else complete the task? What, exactly. Maybe the objective can be accomplished some other way?

Problem: No, he must be there himself. It is an important one time only event (a funeral, a meeting, etc.)

And so on, thinking up preemption strategies for each new problem.

So there we have a brief look at three orthodox, accepted principles of customer service and four concepts from outside the arena of business theory proper that are often quite useful in customer service situations. Hopefully, by continuing to blend accepted principles and ideas with new ones, we can continue to widen our circle of understanding and thus serve our customers in more and more ways.

Peter Quinones

Peter Quinones has had a long career in sales and training. In the early 1990s he headed the field operations for a major research firm and traveled the country training thousands of market researchers. Peter is the author of the Dream Factory, published in 2002, and will be featured in an upcoming volume of Mission Possible with Les Brown and Warren Bennis. He has been elected to one of the major sales guilds in the United States six times and is one of a handful of elite Ebay sellers who has maintained a perfect 100% feedback score after hundreds of transactions.

Peter Quinones
PO Box 478
Brooklyn, NY 11203
Phone: 917.941.2387
Email: pqq@compuserve.com
Web: www.peterq.net

Chapter Twelve

A Commitment to
Customer Service *Excellence*

Richard Tyler

Excellence in business—or for that matter, in anything—must begin with a *commitment* to excellence. No one stumbles into excellence; it is something that is achieved only after there is a commitment, a mental determination to accept *only* excellence, no matter how difficult, no matter how uncomfortable and no matter how stressful the journey may be. The decision to go beyond just being good at what we do drives distance between those organizations truly committed to excellence and everyone else.

Take a moment to think of one of your favorite companies. Now think of two or three sentences to describe that company. Chances are you described your favorite company in terms of the excellent customer service you receive: "Their flights are on time," "They gladly give me a refund," "They do what they say they'll do" and so on.

Although no one has trouble distinguishing between good customer service and bad customer service, simply demonstrating good customer service is not enough to create or keep a competitive advantage. This is because customers *expect* good service. Think of it as the investment for entry, a threshold requirement necessary to play the game. To achieve excellence in business, a company must move from good to excellent customer service. Excellent customer service creates a competitive advantage that is difficult to imitate and becomes a positive point of differentiation.

So how do you create an environment of excellent customer service? We have invested a great deal of time searching for the answer to this question, and through years of our own research and the research of others, we've discovered **20 Customer Service Truths.** Commit to applying the lessons that these truths teach, and you will be well on your way to creating customer service excellence and with it, a lasting competitive advantage.

Customer Service Truth #1:

Poor service is the number one reason companies lose business. Nearly seventy percent of customers who stop doing business with a company do so because of poor service.

Think about the time and money you invest attracting a new customer. Then consider what this simple truth reveals: Despite all of our hand-wringing over how our customers will respond to such external factors as the competition's lower prices or new product introductions, most of the customers that leave us do so because we chase them away!

Early in my career, I worked selling fashion jewelry and other items to gift shops. When I joined the company, the best salesperson was Nicholi. I admired Nicholi's sales performance and enjoyed competing with him for the top sales position. Month after month, he and I would be number one or number two in sales. At first, Nicholi held the number one spot more often than I. But over time, I secured the top spot as often as Nicholi and eventually, more often. As my sales continued a steady growth rate, I started to notice that Nicholi's sales began to level off then decline. It wasn't long before Nicholi slipped to number three, then four and then five just before he left the company.

After he left, I picked up portions of his territory and quickly learned what had happened. I discovered that Nicholi was the salesforce equivalent of a one-hit wonder. He had the ability to go into a new customer and almost always make the first sale. Nicholi knew well how to *sell* the customer. What he didn't understand was how to *serve* the customer. He didn't take the time to understand his customers' wants and needs and over time would lose those customers. While I was able to build my sales base with repeat business and new business, Nicholi was left to survive almost exclusively on only new business. He didn't understand the lesson of **Customer Service Truth #1**, which is that if you want your business to grow long term, you must *add* and *retain* customers.

Customer Service Truth #2:
Seventy-five percent of the customers who stop doing business with a company make no attempt to tell the firm why.

Research from TARP, a world leader in customer service research, reveals that seventy-five of every 100 customers a company loses will never tell the company why they left for the competition. This is a very disturbing statistic, because if you don't know why your customers leave you, you can't correct the problem that caused them to leave.

You risk making the same mistake over and over again without ever knowing it. The lesson in **Customer Service Truth #2** is that if you are committed to excellent customer service, you will develop and implement a system for identifying customer concerns while they can still be fixed (i.e., before the customer walks away). We'll talk more about this later in the chapter.

Customer Service Truth #3:
Ninety-five percent of dissatisfied customers never complain to management or headquarters. Fifty percent never complain at all.

These statistics from the United States Department of Labor and TARP prompt the question, "If customers are dissatisfied, why don't they complain?" We find that there are three main reasons. First, customers don't feel it's worth their time. Most poor customer service experiences steal precious time from the customer. Sticking around to complain about it only wastes more time. Just think about your own experiences. Recall a time when you were stuck in line waiting to check your luggage before a flight. Imagine waiting in line for an hour because of very slow service. When you finally get to the counter, the only thing on your mind is "Get me out of here—I've got a flight to catch!" You're not going to invest more time trying to locate the supervisor to discuss your dissatisfaction. So, over time, given enough bad experiences, we finally say, "Enough is enough," and we take our business elsewhere without ever bothering to tell the company why.

Second, dissatisfied customers don't think company personnel will listen to complaints or do anything about them even if they did listen. The typical customer thinks, "Even if I did complain, no one would do anything about it. If they really cared about the customer, I wouldn't be waiting in this line at all!"

Third, the customer has no easy way to complain. In other words, the company makes the process of complaining cumbersome enough that the effort to complain is too much trouble. Most employees don't want to hear complaints. A customer complaint may mean a poor performance review or worse. So complaint forms are not readily available, and employees tell dissatisfied customers, "You'll have to speak with the manager" (who, of course, has that day off). They do not encourage complaints, and therefore, the "company" rarely hears them.

The company committed to excellent customer service sets itself apart by encouraging customers to discuss their poor-service experiences and by rewarding employees who do something about it. These companies understand that the customer is the most valuable resource for determining what needs to change. They not only encourage customer complaints, they view them as the oxygen required to constantly improve their ability to service their customers' wants and needs.

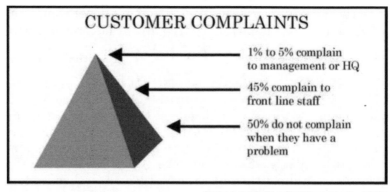

CUSTOMER COMPLAINTS

1% to 5% complain to management or HQ

45% complain to front line staff

50% do not complain when they have a problem

Data provided by TARP research - 1999.

Customer Service Truth #4:
The average dissatisfied customer tells nine to ten others about his or her dissatisfaction.

It's bad enough to fail with one customer; you certainly don't need that experience recounted (and embellished) to ten others. But this is exactly what happens. Unfortunately for some companies, there are dissatisfied customers like me who won't stop at sharing their experience with just ten people. I'm happy to provide an example.

A few years ago, I had several bad experiences with a particular rental car company. On two occasions, I reserved a specific make and model car. The type of vehicle was very important, because I was going to be transporting my mother, who used a wheelchair. On both occasions, I was told that the vehicle I wanted was available and would be ready when I arrived. On both occasions, the vehicle was not ready. In fact, it was apparently not even available! Despite my patient attempts to make the company aware of my experiences, the best response I received (and this came from the head of the company's customer relations department) ended something like this: "I'm having a little difficulty understanding the validity of your complaint." There was never an attempt to understand my concern, let alone rectify it. I ended the conversation with this particular customer relations professional by introducing my company. I explained to her that through my company's seminar programs, consulting and speaking engagements, we have the opportunity to influence thousands of professionals every year. I explained that not only are most of these professionals very interested in hearing stories about customer service, but they travel extensively. I pointed out that I felt compelled to share this experience. Even after providing this information, nothing was done. This company has lost more than $100,000 in business from my company over the years and undoubtedly much more from the people who have heard my story.

The real tragedy is that as a customer, I would have been easy to satisfy. The company needed to understand my wants and needs and then take appropriate action. Talking to a customer about his or her complaint is of no value if your goal is not to resolve the complaint, given that a reasonable and timely resolution is possible.

The lesson of **Customer Service Truth #4** is that those companies committed to excellent customer service respond to one customer's bad experience as if they are saving the business of ten, fifty or 100 customers. Of course, that is because they are!

Customer Service Truth #5:
A satisfied customer tells an average of only five people about his or her good experience.

You may be thinking, "That's not fair! If my company satisfies the customer, why wouldn't that customer want to let more people know about it?" Well, remember what we said at the outset of this chapter. Customers *expect* good service. So there's little to talk about if you are simply meeting expectations. However, when you significantly fall short of expectations or significantly exceed expectations, you create news worthy of discussion.

> "Customers *expect* good service."

So what does this **Customer Service Truth** teach us? First, the old adage that bad news travels fast is true. In this case, bad news travels twice as fast as good news. Second, if there are twice as many people saying bad things about your business than there are saying good things, sooner or later, you'll be out of business. And third, if you want your customers to recommend your company to more than just a few people, you're going to have to provide excellent customer service.

Customer Service Truth #6:
According to the research of noted management expert and author Tom Peters, it takes $10 of new business to replace $1 of lost business.

This means that every time you lose a customer, you have to go out and find $10 worth of business for every dollar that you lost—just to get back to where you started. This may be startling at first, but it makes perfect sense. Think about the effort you put into attracting a new customer—the advertising investment, the research investment, the sales calls, rapport-building efforts, etc. When you are going through that exercise, you're not thinking about only one sale. You're thinking about the long-term relationship and the value of the customer's business over the long haul. You don't mind the effort and investment up front, because you're thinking about how much easier the repeat business will come once the customer has been with you for a while. You don't mind it, that is, until you lose a customer and have to do ten times the work to make up for the lost business.

There are a lot of reasons to develop the habits necessary to creating a "culture of excellence" in customer service. There are few that are more compelling.

Customer Service Truth #7:
It costs between five and ten times as much to attract a new customer as it does to keep an existing one.

This **Customer Service Truth** makes clear that the up-front investment to attract a new customer is expensive—far more expensive, in fact, than the investment necessary to keep existing customers. This, too, makes perfect sense once you understand the concept of switching costs.

> **"...a 5% increase in customer retention can**

Switching costs are those costs a customer incurs when switching from one provider to another. Think about your personal bank. Let's say you receive your monthly bank statement, and you discover an error that requires three phone calls to get resolved. A few days later, you receive a notice informing you that the bank is increasing the rate it charges its customers for certain routine transactions. A week later, one of the bank's ATM machines improperly processes a transaction and then "eats" your ATM card—three more phone calls and two trips to the bank. Although you certainly have good reason to take your business to another bank, you decide to stick it out. Why? Switching costs.

The costs for you to switch from one bank to another are significant. You have to take the time to go to a branch to open a new account, transfer money from one account to the other, close the old account, get new checks printed, apply for a new ATM card, locate the new bank's ATM machines, learn the new bank's policies, account options and fee structure, begin building new relationships with the employees and so on. The whole process of moving your account can seem so time-consuming and cumbersome that you'd rather just put up with poor customer service from you current bank—to a point, of course.

This **Customer Service Truth** teaches us that switching costs work in our favor when we're investing in excellent customer service. They work against us when we're trying to make up for lost business.

Customer Service Truth #8:

The more similar products and prices are, the more quality of service differentiates one business from another.

In many industries, the differences among products and pricing are small. In speaking with professionals from companies within various industries, I often hear the complaint, "There's not a lot I can do to differentiate my business. Our product lines and pricing are so similar to that of our competition that we're practically in a commodities market." I love hearing this, because it gives me a chance to share one of my favorite customer service experiences.

A couple of years ago, I was in the Washington, D.C. area and decided to browse a Nordstrom's department store. I met a young man working in the shoe department who encouraged me to consider a certain brand of shoe. This was a tough sell, because it was not the brand of shoe I had invested in and worn my entire professional career. He said, "I realize these are different than what you are accustomed to, but I really believe that you will be impressed with the way they look on your foot and the way they feel." I put them on, and indeed, I was impressed. I decided to get the shoes. In casual conversation during our time together, the young man asked me how often I made it to D.C. I told him about once a month. He asked me if I visited this particular store when I came to town. I told him that I did so occasionally. He then noted the day of the week and time of the month I was most likely to be in the store.

Six months later, I returned to the store. As I approached the shoe department, I heard from the opposite end of the department,

"Hello, Mr. Tyler. Great to see you again!" Of course, it was the young man who sold me the shoes. How do you think that made me feel? It made me feel like a valued customer. This young man created a simple system that helped him anticipate who he might be seeing in the store on any particular day. Because I told him when I was in town and that I would most likely visit the store on the weekend of the second week of the month, he could anticipate when he might see me again. Even though it had been months since I had seen him, his commitment to excellent customer service ensured that he was prepared for my visit. His personal method of differentiation allowed his company to serve my wants and needs. I ultimately left the store that day with two new pairs of shoes, two new suits and three new ties.

Customer Service Truth #8 teaches us that the opportunities to differentiate your business are around you every day. It might be the language that you use, the look of your facility, the cleanliness of your operation, the training program that results in consistent employee professionalism or a new procedure that cuts customer wait time in half. Commit to investing at least one hour per week coming up with ways to differentiate your business, and you will have already established a competitive advantage.

Customer Service Truth #9:
The tone and first impression of a relationship are established in the first sixty seconds of a meeting.

Cavett Robert, one of the founders of the National Speakers Association—of which I am a proud member—coined the phrase, "You get only one brief chance to make a good first impression." It's true; what happens in the first sixty seconds of a customer's experience with your company sets the tone for the rest of the relationship. That first experience is difficult to forget. If it's a good one, your customer may forgive a slip-up here or there. If the experience is a bad one, there's a good chance you won't have an opportunity to get to know that customer.

In an ideal world, before doing business with a particular company, a customer would have all available information about that company. The customer would have a complete background on all employees, all available product specs, complete company financials from the company's first year in business, a complete profile of the experience of every other customer and so on. And in this ideal world, before making an investment decision, the customer would have enough time to effectively evaluate all this information and compare it against similar data from the company's competitors. But since customers don't live in an ideal world, they neither expect nor want that much information. Instead, customers make decisions on less-than-perfect information.

> "You get only one brief chance to make a

In the absence of complete information, each of us has developed a subconscious system to help quickly process information and make decisions. Often called heuristics, these customized rules of thumb help us efficiently process the thousands of decisions we face every day. A friendly face, a rushed clerk, a poorly lit store front, a pleasant smell, a polished presentation, a poorly written letter are the kinds of clues that we use to make decisions about a company in that first sixty-second exposure. Once we make that initial decision, we subconsciously search for evidence to support our opinion, and we subconsciously overlook or dismiss as an anomaly the evidence that might otherwise work to change our opinion.

This **Customer Service Truth** teaches us that we need to scrutinize *every* detail of the first-contact environment if we are to turn that interaction into our advantage.

Customer Service Truth #10:

Each time customers come in contact with a different company employee for the first time, they form a new impression—of that employee and your company.

Companies too often overlook this important truth. Although that first contact is critical, every subsequent contact works to reeducate the customer about your business. You've taken to heart **Customer Service Truth #9** and scrutinized that first-contact experience to ensure that the customer has a great first impression. But are you aware of the obstacles that diminish the quality of the customer experience once he or she is doing business with you?

Start with your phone system. Does the person calling your company always get a person within a couple of rings? Or do you have an automated system that requires the customer to navigate a series of automated menus? I recently called a company and spent five minutes navigating automated menus only to be dumped into someone's voice mail. Five minutes is a very long time to spend trying to find someone. It's the equivalent of putting someone on hold for five minutes. Wouldn't you agree that putting someone on hold for five minutes is unacceptable?

Your takeaway from **Customer Service Truth #10** is this: Establish the habit of experiencing your company the way your customer does. Make it a point to call your company's customer service line as a customer, spend time navigating your Web site, shop your stores, assemble your products, help a customer receive one of your shipments, whatever it takes to put yourself in your customers' shoes. Pay close attention to the points of impression to make sure the result is excellent customer service.

Remember that if your customers like you, they can be very forgiving, but subconsciously, the result of every interaction adds up. If you tip the balance to the negative, it is the start of a real landslide.

Customer Service Truth #11:
The same attitude that leads to increased customer satisfaction leads to increased employee performance.

Remember that you have external and internal (employee) customers; you need to provide both with excellent service. Nothing undermines a customer-service-excellence strategy faster than poor internal customer service. A company can embrace the idea of excellence in customer service, create catchy tag lines, make big promises and truly believe that implementing such a program is the right thing to do. But if the company does not have a team committed to delivering on those promises, there simply is no program.

Employees are always the first to sniff out a phony initiative. They are skeptical by nature and for good reason. The implementation rate of popular corporate initiatives is dizzying—as is the rate of senior-management turnover. So as you begin discussing excellence in customer service on the heels of your company's latest Pseudo-Classic Feng Shui Quality Triangulation Performance Improvement Initiative, understand that your employees may be looking for proof of your resolve. They'll find that resolve if your commitment to customer service excellence is as apparent to internal customers as it is to external customers.

Recently, a major computer company hired a new CEO to heal a bleeding balance sheet. By all accounts, this new CEO took his job seriously and upon assuming the post, sent out the following policy statement to his employees:

> "If you have a desire to meet with me to discuss any concerns you may have, send such requests to my secretary in writing. She has been instructed to schedule up to five appointments on the first and third Thursday mornings of each month to discuss such issues. Appointments will be scheduled on a first-come-first-served basis. I encourage you to make your request early so that I may get to it within a reasonable period of time during the year."

With this one communication, the CEO put up a psychological barrier that sent a strong message to his employees: *"I don't care what your concerns are; you are the reason this company is in trouble. I do not want to hear from you."* It will not come as a surprise that he didn't last long.

The lesson: Your employees are your company. If they are committed to excellence in customer service, your company will earn a competitive advantage.

Customer Service Truth #12:

Customers pay more for better service—ten percent more on an undifferentiated product or service, according to a study conducted for the American Society for Quality Control. Customers also pay with loyalties.

Why are customers willing to invest more for better service? It is a simple matter of supply and demand. In every industry, the supply of companies providing better service is low. When you provide excellent customer service, your customers will be willing to invest more for it. Think back to my Nordstrom example. When I invested $3,500 in new clothing that day, I *knew* that my investment for the same products could have been lower at another store. But don't you think that the service I received was worth the additional investment? I certainly did. The service I received from the Nordstrom staff allowed me to make quality decisions about products I needed in a way that was quick and convenient. Because of their commitment to excellent customer service, I saved time and money. I didn't have to go to multiple outlets evaluating a wide variety of options before finding what I needed. *That's* the kind of service that people *remember* and *reward*.

> **Customers who receive excellent customer**

The reward that you receive because of excellent customer service goes well beyond the additional investment the customer is willing to make in a single transaction. Customers who receive excellent customer service will also reward your company with a highly desirable commodity—their loyalty. Research reveals that when it comes to switching from one business to another, service is five times more important than any other factor. Commit to developing the habits that will result in excellent customer service, and you will keep more of your current customers while you gain more new ones.

Customer Service Truth #13:

Ninety-five percent of dissatisfied customers would do business again with a company if their problems were solved quickly and satisfactorily—greater loyalty than if they had no problems at all.

This truth teaches us that if you have dissatisfied customers and you satisfy their concerns quickly, their loyalty to your company will increase significantly. They will be more loyal to you, in fact, than if they never had problems at all.

Although customers expect to receive good customer service, they are not surprised when they don't get it. Poor customer service is served up in too many doses per day for it to catch anyone off guard. And of course, no company, regardless of how committed it is to providing excellent customer service, is immune from occasionally mishandling a customer interaction. The question is, "*How* does the company handle the shortfall?"

The company that understands the lesson within this truth responds to the customer's dissatisfaction by meeting the customer's wants and needs quickly. Again, consider your own experience. Think of a time when you had a service concern satisfied quickly. Have you ever told someone about it? Have you ever found yourself saying, "I had a problem with that company, but they fixed it right away. They are really good to deal with. I'm definitely going to continue doing business with them."

The fact that a company stumbles is not at all a surprise; but when the company quickly and consistently springs to its feet to address a customer dissatisfaction, that's a positive point of differentiation that gets rewarded with increased loyalty. This truth teaches us that a customer *problem* really is an *opportunity*, if we look at it that way.

Customer Service Truth #14:

Excellent customer service must be a way of life for every employee up and down the corporate ladder. The person who talks to the customer should have the power to satisfy the customer.

Consider again my rental-car-company experience. The employees who were hired to talk to customers didn't have the authority or power to satisfy my simple concern. Even the *head* of the customer relations department did not have the power to satisfy my concern! A company should never ask an employee to speak with a dissatisfied customer if that employee is not empowered to satisfy the customer. Doing so simply results in a more dissatisfied—potentially angry—ex-customer (the kind that likes to tell people about the experience). If the customer spends the time to complain about a bad experience he or she had with your company, don't make the customer tell the story to the front-line customer service representative, the group supervisor, the department manager and then the department director, just to be told that "there's nothing we can do."

The companies that are committed to excellent customer service have established a proven process to ensure that someone is empowered to listen to and acknowledge customers' concerns and do something about them. This doesn't mean every customer with a concern should get whatever he or she wants. It does mean that you should have your best employees in these roles, and they should have authority to take immediate action. If they need help handling a particular customer situation, then make sure the call doesn't get escalated more than once. That is, make sure whoever is brought in to assist your customer relations professional has final authority to take reasonable steps to satisfy the customer.

Customer Service Truth #15:
All employees are involved in sales. Excellent sales require excellent service.

Not long ago, a Fortune 500 company engaged my services as the Keynote Speaker at their annual meeting. The topic was "Powerful Leadership—The Key to Success." The meeting was held at a luxury hotel. I pulled my car to the front door, got out, grabbed some bags and headed toward the door with my arms full. I needed help getting everything through the door, but no one was around to notice. When I finally got through the door, I saw the hotel's doorman a few feet away, chatting with the concierge. I couldn't pass up the opportunity to investigate this customer service situation. Approaching the two hotel employees, I said, "I'm staying at your hotel this evening, and I'd like to know if you offer your guests all-night room service." The doorman said, "I don't know. I just work the door." Resisting the temptation to explore that particular discrepancy, I turned to the concierge and asked, "Do you know if the hotel offers all-night room service?" "I don't know. I'm new" he said. "You'll have to ask at the front desk." Neither employee offered to help with my bags or find the answer to my question.

Regardless of how much this hotel invested in construction, marketing, advertising, room amenities, lobby décor or service offerings, my impression of the hotel was most influenced by one five-minute interaction with two employees. To achieve excellent sales, your employees must be providing excellent customer service. **Customer Service Truth #15** teaches us that all of our employees are salespeople, and as such, they must receive regular, quality training— training in professional sales skills, training in product (service) knowledge, training in customer service and training about what to do when they don't know the answer.

Customer Service Truth #16:
Excellent service leads to increased sales.

Guaranteed sustainable sales performance comes as a result of a commitment to excellent customer service. If your company is consistently providing excellent customer service, then you are already reaping the proven rewards that positive differentiation delivers. However, if your company is not consistently providing the level of customer service that you believe is possible, then you have an excellent opportunity.

Differentiating your company on the basis of excellent customer service is the best investment you can make. When compared to other forms of differentiation, such as product-based differentiation, improving customer service doesn't require sophisticated research and development, product development, re-tooling or new advertising campaigns. Best of all, you have a head start, because your employees already know a lot about excellent customer service. They know about it, because at some point in their lives, they have experienced it, and they remember it. Establishing a trustworthy framework is usually all that is necessary to release the creative energy that your employees already possess and want to use. By the way, you get this creative energy for FREE.

I once heard a story about the dramatic impact of establishing such a framework—and it involved my old friend, Nordstrom. Many of you have experienced Nordstrom's excellent customer service firsthand. But what you experienced was the *result* of a commitment to customer service excellence that started with a trustworthy framework, the backbone of which is an employee training program. One aspect of Nordstrom's program is the requirement that an employee never use such negative language as, "No," "We can't do that," etc. As a test to a newly-trained employee's grasp of the material, a customer appeared in a Nordstrom store wanting to return four car tires that weren't the correct size for his car. Since Nordstrom doesn't sell tires, the employee was faced with quite a dilemma! To tell the customer that he couldn't return the tires to Nordstrom would be using language inconsistent with the commitment to customer service excellence he learned in his training. So after taking a moment to fully understand the customer's concern and his needs, the employee asked the man if he would leave the tires and give him about an hour to "sort things out." The customer agreed. The employee took the tires to a local tire shop, traded them in for the correct size, returned to the store within an hour and satisfied the customer.

The commitment to excellence that Nordstrom demonstrated through training and empowering its employees resulted in a creative solution that would be unthinkable in most any other organization. The lesson in this **Customer Service Truth** is that unlocking the excellent customer service capabilities within each of your employees translates into a key point of differentiation that delivers *sustainable* revenue increases.

Customer Service Truth #17:

Companies should pay attention to how they spend money. Overspending in some areas may mean you're underspending in customer service, thereby losing business.

Can you think of an example where your company spent too much money on something that was not critical to the company's mission? In the time it took you to get from the last sentence to this one, you probably came up with about five examples, right? It is a truism of all businesses: We often overspend on things that are ultimately unimportant. While this is not inherently catastrophic (depending, of course, on *how much* we overspend), the danger is that overspending on the wrong things usually has a partner: underspending on the right things.

If you asked employees in your organization how committed your company was to its customers, I predict you would hear statements like, "The customer is king," "We're 100-percent committed to our customers," "Our first purpose is to serve our customers" and so on. If you then listed the ways your company supports your employees' enthusiasm, you might quickly see a glaring inconsistency. Don't despair; you're not alone. The unfortunate fact is that despite all of our rhetoric about the value of our customers, the average American company invests only $3 per employee in annual customer service education. That's right, just three dollars set aside to improve the one thing that we all agree is most important. Investments by most companies that are not American are in the same range or lower.

There is no magical dollar amount that separates those companies committed to customer service excellence from all the others, because companies' needs are different. But I can tell you that if your company is only spending $3 per employee on customer service education, you are wasting your money. Achieving customer service excellence takes more than that. Commitment to customer service excellence means developing a framework that becomes a part of the company's culture. It means viewing all of your employees as salespeople and giving them the tools they need to become true advocates for your customers. It means understanding that providing customer service is not intuitive for everyone and that it requires consistent, high-quality training. A recent study by Reid Systems illustrates this particular point:

- Forty-five percent of employees surveyed said they believe that customers should be told when they are wrong.
- Forty-six percent said customers have to follow the rules if they are going to get help.
- Thirty-four percent said they would prefer to work behind the scenes rather than with customers.

If the above statistics are applicable to your workforce, wouldn't you agree that it will take more than $3 per employee to achieve excellent customer service? I believe there is great news in these numbers. Just imagine that these statistics apply to your competition. What an excellent opportunity you have to gain a sustainable strategic advantage!

Customer Service Truth #17 teaches us that investing in professional service and professional sales-skill training is every bit as important to growth and profitability as anything else we can do; and *it is more important than most things we do.* Invest in training your people first and continually if you want to put and keep your customer first.

Customer Service Truth #18:
Customers invest in the whole experience.

As customers, when we choose a particular company with which to do business, it is for more than just one reason. It's a combination of features and characteristics that lead us into the relationship. Once we are in the relationship, we invest in the whole experience.

This truth teaches two critical lessons: First, once you recognize that your customers are investing in the entire experience, you will begin to see many ways to strengthen the customer relationship. Take, for example, a big-box retail store in a strip center. The store manager of the retail store may focus extraordinary amounts of time ensuring that the store is merchandised perfectly and that the employees are highly trained to maximize the customers' time. If the store manager understands that the customer who chooses to shop in the store is investing in the entire experience and not just location, product and price, then the manager will look for ways to strengthen that relationship at every point of contact. The manager might improve the lighting in the parking lot, offer valet parking and provide benches throughout the store for customers to sit down and so on.

The second critical lesson within this truth is that any disconnect in the relationship can cost you customers, so you must understand that relationship. I will give you a personal example. There is a particular department store that I visit often. Over the years, I have built a relationship with this company, and consequently, I regularly invest with them. My investing pattern has resulted in membership in the store's preferred shopping club, which provides certain benefits that I find useful.

One Saturday, I was shopping in the store, and I stopped for a moment in the domestics department. I decided to sit on the corner of a display bed. Before long, a young clerk approached me:

"Sir, you can't sit there."

I explained that I was just resting for a moment and that I would be sure to not upset the display.

"I'm sorry, sir. You must get up," She persisted.

I looked at her, sighed and said, "Okay." I have not been back in that store since and will not return. This store lost a customer that was regularly investing more than $10,000 per year with them and has never bothered to follow up to find out why.

The lesson of **Customer Service Truth #18** is that if you understand that your customers are with you because of the entire experience, you will understand that the relationship can be fragile. You can use this to your advantage to strengthen your relationship, or you can ignore it and risk losing your best customers.

Customer Service Truth #19:
Excellent companies remember to say "thank you."

A thank-you may seem trivial—an unnecessary nicety. Let your competition believe that while you demonstrate to your customers that you don't take them for granted.

Excellent companies understand the power in saying "thank you" at the right times. They recognize the customers' efforts in ways that appeal to the customer's deepest human desires—to feel loved, wanted, needed and important.

There are five times when your employees should always thank a customer other than at the point of sale (i.e., "Thank you for shopping with us today."):

1. **When the customer takes on a new product or service**: When your customer invests in new products or services, the customer is sending a strong message that they believe in the relationship and want to extend it. Make sure you recognize that vote of confidence in your company.

2. **When the customer offers a suggestion**: How often do you offer a suggestion to an employee who simply stares back at you like you just asked them to divide the square root of twenty-three by the distance between the sun and the moon? It's not the employee's fault if they've never been told how to handle a customer suggestion; it's the company's responsibility to teach employees how to respond. And it certainly doesn't have to be much. If the person receiving the suggestion is not a decision maker, all they have to say is something simple like, "That's a very interesting idea. I'd like to bring this up to my manager. Thank you for taking the time to share it." You should be delighted when a customer provides suggestions. Can you think of a better source of information to provide insight into how to improve your service to that person?

3. **When the customer provides a referral, brings a new customer to you, provides a good lead, etc.**: We all antici-

pate that if we provide excellent customer service, we'll benefit from referral business. Unfortunately, we too often act like we deserve it and therefore don't consider saying thank-you to those that bring it to us. By letting your customers know how much you appreciate their loyalty and recommendations, you will strengthen the relationship and get even more referrals and recommendations.

4. **When he or she provides a compliment**: We too often believe that we must deflect the compliment out of modesty. That can backfire in a very big way if your customer believes you devalue his or her opinion. When you deflect a customer's compliment, it's like saying, "You're wrong." In any other context, the excellent company would never do that, so don't do it here.

5. **When the customer complains**: When customers complain, they are telling you that you are not meeting their wants and needs. Take the opportunity to tell them how much you appreciate their feedback even after being disappointed. It will not only help disarm them and diffuse the situation, but it will provide you with key insight into how you can improve your business. Thank the customer for giving you that opportunity.

Customer Service Truth #19 teaches us that the simple gestures are often the most powerful ways to build and strengthen customer relationships.

Customer Service Truth #20:
Customers will tell a company where it needs improvement,
but most companies will not take advantage of this feedback.

When was the last time you talked with your customers about how well your company was serving their needs—not through a face-less questionnaire but real, personal communication? Once again, consider the investment your company makes to attract a new customer. You may invest in expensive advertising: investing a lot of time and money conducting research, making multiple, in-person presentations and follow-up phone calls and preparing letters and proposals. Now consider how much time you invest in keeping those customers. Based on the lessons the **20 Customer Service Truths** teach us, wouldn't you agree that the excellent customer service organization is just as committed to keeping the customer as it is to attracting the customer? Wouldn't you also agree that NOW is the time to begin turning these lessons into your competitive advantage?

I challenge you to take action right now. Get up now and get your calendar, a pen and piece of paper.

- Write down the names of your top ten, fifteen or twenty customers. If your organization has many thousands of regular customers (e.g. a retailer), write down the names of at least fifteen customers that you know. Depending on your position within your organization, your list may be from the customers you serve in your particular region. If you are an Internet-only company, your customers may be other Web-based firms.
- Get out your calendar and schedule thirty minutes for each of the identified customers. Schedule the first appointment no later than tomorrow.
- Commit to getting real customer service feedback using the following as a guide:
    - Call or visit the customers on your list and explain that you are very interested in getting genuine feedback on how well your company is meeting their wants and needs. If your only

method of contacting your customers is via the Web, use e-mail or a brief Web-site survey.

o   Tell these customers that you are contacting them specifically because you value their opinions and you know you can count on them to provide no-nonsense, candid feedback.

o   Actively listen to their concerns. That is, through your actions, make it clear that your customers' concerns are valuable and that you intend to do something about them. Take notes and rephrase the concerns back to the customers to make sure you understand what they are saying.

o   Commit to following up on the concerns, and then do it quickly! Whether through a follow-up phone call, letter or e-mail (as appropriate), repeat the customers' concerns and then let the customers know what you have done or are doing about improving your service to them. Encourage the customers to contact you any time to provide additional feedback.

Case in point . . .

A friend of mine recently told me about one of his clients, a billion dollar company in the paper industry. He was working with the company to develop a customer communications strategy that would result in regular customer-service feedback. The client was dragging its feet on implementing this process when, without warning, it lost one of its biggest and longest-standing customers (and with it, millions of dollars in annual revenue). As the company struggled to determine what happened, it learned that over time there had been several customer service issues that had not been addressed satisfactorily.

These issues never "bubbled to the top" where they would certainly have been addressed, and a competitor seized the opportunity to satisfy the customer's wants and needs. The customer communications program was quickly implemented, but what a shame. It took a devastating loss to get the company to understand how important it is to focus at least as much time and energy on keeping the customer as it did attracting the customer. How many of your customers are preparing right now to walk away from you?

Two other points: First, unless it will stifle candid feedback, bring two or three key members of your team with you when you call or visit the customers on your list. This serves two purposes: It will make it clear to your team that you are serious about this process, and it will teach them how to effectively implement it. Second, make sure this process doesn't happen only once. Make this a routine that becomes a hallmark of your organization. Because most people will make excuses for not committing to this process, you will have a key competitive advantage.

This investment of your time will pay you back many times over. This seemingly simple process, consistently practiced, *will* separate the good from the *excellent*. And as a result, you will not only lose fewer customers, your excellent customer service will earn you additional business.

I leave you with one more thought: When it comes to sales, when it comes to customer service, when it comes to input from your people and from your customers:

"Remember, your success tomorrow is in direct proportion to your 'Commitment to *EXCELLENCE*™' today."™

Richard Tyler

Richard Tyler is CEO of **Richard Tyler International, Inc.™** an organization named one of the top 50 training and consulting firms in the world. Mr. Tyler's success in sales, quality improvement, management and customer service and his reputation for powerful educational methods and motivational techniques, have made him one of the most sought after consultants, lecturers and teachers. Mr. Tyler shares his philosophies with millions of individuals each year through keynote speaking, syndicated writing, radio, television, seminars, books and tapes.

Mr. Tyler's book *"SMART BUSINESS STRATEGIES*™, *The* **Guide to Small Business Marketing** *EXCELLENCE"* is being hailed as one of the best books ever written for small-business marketing. His philosophies have been featured in *Entrepreneur Magazine*® as well as in hundreds of articles and interviews.

Mr. Tyler is the founder of the **LEADERSHIP FOR TOMORROW™**, an organization dedicated to educating young adults in the importance of **self-esteem, goal setting** and **life-long success.** He also serves as a board member to such community organizations as **Be An Angel Fund, Inc.**, a non-profit organization helping multiple handicapped and profoundly deaf children to have a better life.

Richard Tyler International, Inc.™
P.O. BOX 630249
Houston, TX 77263-0249
Phone: 713-974-7214
Email: RichardTyler@RichardTyler.com
Websites: www.RichardTyler.com
             www.TylerTraining.com
             www.ExcellenceEdge.com